The Market Research and Insight Yearbook

The Market Research and Insight Yearbook

Transforming evidence into impact

70 years of helping
people talk to power

LONDON PHILADELPHIA NEW DELHI

First published in Great Britain and the United States in 2016 by the Market Research Society

2nd Floor, 45 Gee Street	1518 Walnut Street, Suite 1100	4737/23 Ansari Road
London	Philadelphia PA 19102	Daryaganj
EC1V 3RS	USA	New Delhi 110002
United Kingdom		India

© Market Research Society 2016

ISBN   978 0 7494 7833 9
E-ISBN   978 0 7494 7834 6

British Library Cataloguing-in-Publication Data

A CIP record for this book is available from the British Library.

Typeset by Graphicraft Limited, Hong Kong
Print production managed by Jellyfish
Printed and bound in the UK by Henry Ling Limited at the Dorset Press, Dorchester DT1 1HD

IN BRIEF

CONTENTS

FIGURES AND TABLES

The Ark

Contact:

The Ark
Unit 1
Old Barn
Wicklesham Lodge Farm
Fargindon
Oxon
SN7 7PN

Phone: +44 (0)1367 245 470
E-mail: 2by2@ark-data.co.uk
Website: www.ark-data.co.uk

We are experienced industry professionals who passionately believe the foundation of any successful business depends on the quality of its data and that process starts with having clean, accurate and reliable data. Without this every action and decision taken is potentially flawed.

For these reasons, The Ark launched the National Deceased Register in 2011 and our gone-away file, Re-mover, in 2013 having identified a need in the market for truly reliable suppression data. Both files have now been universally acclaimed to be the most comprehensive accurate and reliable suppression products available on the market.

It's no longer good enough to rely on out dated legacy suppression files that don't deliver the results your business should be demanding.

For more information about our products and the opportunity to evaluate our data for free please do get in touch.

B2B International

B2B International is a specialist business-to-business market research consultancy that provides customized B2B market research and intelligence studies to the world's leading companies. Established in 1998, the company has conducted over 3,000 full-service projects, delivering world-class research to over 600 b2b brands. It is now the largest independently-owned b2b market research company in the world.

The company has office locations across North America, Europe and Asia-Pacific, and has broader in-house capabilities for international projects, having researched over 90 countries in the last 12 months alone.

B2B International has a diverse service portfolio and can assist clients with a range of research challenges. Types of research offered include branding, segmentation, customer experience/'voice of the customer' (VOC), product and pricing research, competitor intelligence, markets and opportunities studies and employee surveys. The company has researched every industry vertical, resulting in powerful cross-industry experience that it leverages with each client.

B2B International's mission is to challenge the status quo, 'using skilfully collected evidence to empower b2b brands to grow and reach their full potential. It uses research insights in a commercial context, helping companies to drive tactical and strategic action plans.

Contact:

Conor Wilcock
Research Director
B2B International
Bramhall House
14 Ack Lane East
Bramhall
Stockport
Manchester
SK7 2BY

Phone: +44 (0)61 440 6000
E-mail: conorw@b2binternational.com
Website: www.b2binternational.com

Illuminas

Contact:

John Connaughton
CEO
Illuminas
183 Eversholt St
London
NW1 1BU

Phone: +44 (0)20 7909 0935
Mobile: +44 (0)7946 277 959
E-mail: john.connaughton@illuminas.com
Website: www.illuminas.com

Or:
Martin Cary
COO
Illuminas
183 Eversholt St
London
NW1 1BU

Phone: +44 (0)20 7909 0926
Mobile: +44 (0)7793 041 679
E-mail: martin.cary@illuminas.com
Website: www.illuminas.com

Established over 25 years and with more than 75 people in offices in the UK and US, Illuminas provides strategic research across international consumer and B2B markets for leading brands in sectors including technology, finance, retail, healthcare and transport.

We develop custom quantitative and qualitative research solutions that help brands make informed decisions to fuel growth. Our thought leadership and innovative thinking has earned us more than 20 industry awards since our inception.

Illuminas is a partnership, wholly owned and operated by its senior personnel. We are a practitioner-led organization with a professional services business model. Our clients and our people are our only stakeholders.

Ipsos MORI

 Ipsos MORI

Contact:

Ben Page
Chief Executive
Ipsos MORI
3 Thomas More Square
London
E1W 1YW

Phone: +44 (0)20 3059 5000
E-mail: ben.page@ipsos.com
Website: www.ipsos-mori.com

Ipsos MORI, part of the Ipsos group, is one of the UK's largest and most innovative research agencies, working for a wide range of global businesses, the FTSE100 and many government departments and public bodies.

We specialize in solving a range of challenges for our clients, whether these are related to business or consumers, brands or society. Our areas of expertise range from communication, media, innovation, brand and healthcare research through to stakeholder management, corporate reputation and social and political research.

We are passionately curious about people, markets, brands and society. We deliver information, and analysis that makes our complex world easier and faster to navigate and inspires our clients to make smarter decisions.

Jungle Green

Contact:

Janice Guy
Jungle Green mrc
79 Coldharbour Road
Bristol
BS6 7LU

Phone +44 (0)1179 144921
Mobile: +44 (0)7866 897139
E-mail: janice@junglegreenmrc.co.uk
Website: www.junglegreenmrc.co.uk

Jungle Green is a team of senior marketing research associates who have worked together for over 20 years. We specialize in transport research and the health and charitable sectors. We operate nationally from our base in Bristol, with a strong presence in the North and East of England.

The Jungle Green team members who have the early detailed discussions, and put together the research plan and proposal, are the same team members who conduct all of the qualitative research, write the quantitative project materials, organize the fieldwork and conduct the subsequent analysis. They are also the same individuals who will be presenting the research findings at the end of the project. We pride ourselves on having close working relationships with our clients and have been successful in continuing to work with our clients over many years, getting to know them and their organizations in depth.

Market Research Society

70 years of helping people talk to power

Contact:

Market Research Society
The Old Trading House
15 Northburgh Street
London
EC1V 0JR

Phone: +44 (0)20 7490 4911
E-mail: info@mrs.org.uk
Website: www.mrs.org.uk

For 70 years, the Market Research Society (MRS) has been promoting, protecting and connecting the market, social and opinion research sector. MRS regulates individuals and companies in the UK via its membership and accredited company partner schemes.

From a small start in 1946 in a restaurant in Old Compton Street in Soho, London, when an optimal membership number was deemed to be 25, but only 23 individuals were thought to be 'suitable', MRS has grown to represent over 5,000 members in 49 countries and accredit over 500 companies working in the UK and elsewhere.

This year a new report, *The Business of Evidence 2016*, prepared for MRS by PwC, shows that the UK sector has grown by over 60% in GVA to £4.8billion, and with parallel increases in both data analytics and qualitative research. The UK retains a pre-eminent position worldwide.

This growth is predicated on innovation, creativity and trust. These factors depend on skilled, talented, curious, principled people who are the key asset of the sector. MRS helps the creation of this talent pool and has become the world's leading trainer and qualifier in the research sector. This development expertise has helped MRS support initiatives in areas such as Rwanda and Nigeria to provide access to internationally acknowledged research training for young women in these troubled areas.

The new world which marries data analysis and qualitative curation also needs professionalism and an ethical approach to the people whose personal data this all relies upon. The Fair Data mark, which has been developed by MRS, should be a personal commitment from all of us to assure this trust.

Mydex

^mydex

Contact:

David Alexander
CEO
Mydex CIC
Great Wheelers Farm
The Green
Sarratt
Rickmansworth WD3 6BJ

Phone: +44 (0)20 3239 6245
E-mail: david@mydex.org
Website: https://mydex.org

Or:
Jack Mitchell
Head of Communications

Phone: +44 (0)20 7193 7352
E-mail: jack@mydex.org
Website: https://mydex.org

Mydex is a Community Interest Company. It is asset locked. It serves individuals by helping them manage their lives more effectively through provision of tools and services that let them collect, accumulate, organize, analyse and share the data about their lives – whether this is data that organizations hold about them, that they generate themselves, or is generated around them through daily living. In short, we are different, and we focus on trust. Fair Data certification is an important external indicator of our commitment to both of these.

Personal data is valuable, and personal control over personal data requires both transparency and trust. Our mission as a Community Interest Company and operator of a Trust Framework and secure platform is to demonstrate this internally and externally. Certification as a Fair Data Company and the first certified Fair Data Enabler is an important external measure of trust, as is our ISO27001 certification for information security management.

Connecting to the Mydex Platform delivers benefits to the organisation, their customers and the long term relationship they have with each other. It reduces friction in customer journeys, effort for the customer and the organization, and back-office costs in terms of verification, data logistics and achieving compliance.

Mydex acts as a neutral, non-competing, public service platform, and is designed to embed trust in all transactions and interactions between an organization and those they service and support.

Connecting Mydex to existing systems and services is easy and the entire customer journey and brand experience remains with the connecting organization.

Mydex enables organizations to open up new channels of engagement, support omni-channel more easily and access a broader, richer set of timely and accurate information about customers, secure better insights and achieve easier personalisation of services at the same time as assisting in achieving Fair Data certification.

PwC Research to Insight (r2i)

Contact:

Alison Blair
Director
Research to Insight (r2i)
Waterfront Plaza
8 Laganbank Road
Belfast
BT1 3LR

Phone: +44 (0)28 90 415381
E-mail: alison.b.blair@uk.pwc.com
Website: www.pwc.co.uk/r2i
Blog: http://pwc.blogs.com/
    research_to_insight

Research to Insight (r2i) is PwC's global Centre of Excellence for market research. For over 20 years we've undertaken some of the most prestigious and thought-provoking research in Europe, the Americas and Asia Pacific. We offer a full suite of research solutions to deliver insight for global clients. r2i also works closely with the PwC international network to develop cutting-edge Points of View, informed by our industry expertise and business mind set. We use market-leading data visualization tools to help organizations make sense of information and work collaboratively with them to drive actionable insight.

Quadrangle

Customer know-how in a digital world

Contact:

Quadrangle
The Butlers Wharf Building
36 Shad Thames
London
SE1 2YE

Phone: +44 (0)20 7357 9919
E-mail: john.gambles@quadrangle.com
Website: www.quadrangle.com

Digital disrupts.

Over the last few years, it's become increasingly clear how – because of the unprecedented power it is putting in the hands of customers – the second wave of digital is changing the game for clients and agencies alike.

For 20 years our core business was strategic consulting, helping leading brands, multinationals, major plcs and government departments create and execute customer-led strategies.

In 2007, we moved into the research space. Since then we've grown rapidly, worked with amazing clients in the UK and internationally and built a first-rate team. We have also won AURA's Commercial Acumen award three out of the last five years and, currently, are the Research Agency of the Year.

Leveraging our consulting roots, the work we do now centres on helping clients use research and data insight to do two absolutely crucial things:

1 Align customer strategy, putting digital at the heart.

2 Build and deploy customer know-how to create value in a digital world.

Saros Research

Contact:

Maya Middlemiss
Managing Director
Saros Research Ltd
PO Box 71506
London
SE10 1BX

Phone: +44 (0)20 8481 7160
E-mail: maya@sarosresearch.com
Website: www.sarosresearch.com

Saros Research Ltd specializes in participant recruitment for qualitative and user experience research within the UK. Since pioneering the database-driven approach in this market at the turn of the millennium, the Saros team have placed over 25,000 participants in projects ranging from FMCG focus groups to virtual reality testing – and everything in between. Our specialist project management team includes experts in gaming, finance, fashion, children and patient research but all are versatile and ready for the next challenge, and committed to excellence in client service.

Saros Research is dedicated to professionalizing participant recruitment and participant welfare, and created *The Participant Principle: A guide to getting the best recruitment for your user testing and qualitative research* (UPP Books 2016). Sustained investment in database development and marketing outreach brings hundreds of new potential participants into contact with qualitative opportunities every week, and enables the delivery of a recruitment service with integrity and accuracy.

Sparkler

Sparkler is consumer insight and brand strategy consultancy which is designed to help build businesses for the digital age.

We are a full-service, boutique consultancy comprising 50 people across the key disciplines required to build services & brands in the 2016 marketplace. Our services include Consumer Insight, Brand Positioning & Service Innovation. We work primarily with blue-chip companies who are looking to develop their offer across the whole consumer journey, understanding all touchpoints. Our methodologies cover all the usual traditional insight methods, plus a suite of leading edge digital approaches. We have a burgeoning digital communities and panels division.

Contact:

Andy Goll
Sparkler
58-60 Berners Street
London
W1T 3NQ

Phone: +44 (0)20 7079 9555
E-mail: andyg@sparkler.co.uk
Website: www.sparkler.co.uk

Spinach

Spinach

Contact:

Spinach Ltd
144 Liverpool Road
London
N1 1LA

Phone: +44 (0)20 7609 6000
E-mail: info@spinach.co.uk
Website: www.spinach.co.uk

Founded independently in 2002, Spinach is a unique and dynamic London-based agency delivering high standards of UK and international qualitative research, idea generation and training – incorporating purposeful creativity to help transform brands.

We are artful in the way we work and infuse both our projects and our clients with creative thinking. Our two key strengths are co-ordinating multi-market qual studies and working collaboratively to crack tricky strategic and communications issues.

At Spinach we frequently complement and boost qualitative exploration with other disciplines, such as semiotics and psychotherapy. Within our multi-talented team we're particularly proud to have our own Director of Creativity, who is an innovative experiential facilitator, bringing a different kind of thought leadership to the business.

Last year Spinach launched its specialist kids and teens unit, Sprout, to explore and 'create with purpose' in child-centric ways with younger audiences.

If you'd like to learn more about Spinach, Sprout and how we might work together in the future, please visit spinach.co.uk or contact info@spinach.co.uk. We'd be delighted to hear from you.

Trinity McQueen

Contact:

Trinity McQueen London
24 Greville St
Farringdon
London
EC1N 8SS

Phone: +44 (0)20 3008 4482

Or:
Trinity McQueen Leeds
Victoria Wharf (3rd Floor)
4 The Embankment
Sovereign Street
Leeds
LS1 4BA

Phone: +44 (0)113 451 0000

Both sites:
E-mail: hello@trinitymcqueen.com
Website: www.trinitymcqueen.com

Trinity McQueen is a full service insight consultancy that combines original research, sector expertise and strategic thinking. We help clients answer some of the most challenging business questions that today's technology-driven, multi-channel world presents. We started life as the planning team within an advertising agency. Much has changed since those early days but our founding principles of creativity, independence and fresh thinking haven't.

Our formula is simple: we use technology and bespoke, immersive research approaches to get closer to consumers. Our appetite to challenge the status quo and collaborate with clients makes a commercial difference.

Trinity McQueen is proud to be MRS winners and finalists for the last 7 years, including 'Best New Agency'.

FOREWORD
by Dame Dianne Thompson
President, the Market Research Society

In a career spanning over 40 years in marketing roles and senior management, I have consistently championed good research as a key factor in commercial success and evidence-based decision making. I have worked mainly in consumer-facing and marketing service businesses and I believe that knowing your customer is the cornerstone for successful strategies. Research and insight are vital in any business, and that is why I am delighted that MRS, celebrating its 70th year, has published this Yearbook highlighting the power and impact of research.

Research is critical to strategy development and operational effectiveness. The case studies in this Yearbook demonstrate how important research is for organizations seeking to develop their business propositions, increase revenues but also reduce costs, and in the making of investment decisions. The use of research in public policy also continues to evolve as governments increasingly need to understand citizens, supporters and the impacts of their policies.

The opportunities of new and emerging technology and Big Data expand horizons for research but also demand new skills in the areas of integration, reconciliation and interpretation, and places even greater emphasis on the need for researchers to tell the human story behind the data. Big Data needs be smart to be useful, and without context and interpretation it remains just a lot of potentially very expensive numbers.

Asking or challenging decision makers to make life- or business-changing decisions can only be done if the professional standard of research is beyond challenge. There is a high level of creativity, innovation and experimentation being undertaken by researchers, but research can only benefit from these opportunities with a firm understanding of and adherence to ethical requirements, as embodied by the MRS *Code of Conduct* and Fair Data.

Researchers need to know that what they do affects people both at work and in their everyday lives and to take a personal responsibility for the quality of what they deliver.

I strongly recommend those wanting to understand more about the transformative impact of research to read this book.

INTRODUCTION

MRS at 70

As MRS celebrates its 70th year we are delighted to join forces with Kogan Page to produce this inaugural *Market Research and Insight Yearbook: Transforming evidence into impact.*

Transformation is the right word for the current phase for research, and indeed for MRS. Within our first Special Report we reflect back on the past 70 years of research and celebrate some of the important milestones – social, commercial, creative and intellectual – that formed the foundations of today's vibrant research sector.

Bigger and better

The dynamics of the research market are explored in the second Special Report, reporting on the outcome of *The Business of Evidence 2016*, a market assessment project undertaken by PwC on behalf of MRS. The good news is that the research market has grown by over 60 per cent from £3bn GVA in 2012 to £4.8bn GVA in 2016. This transformation has largely been driven by data analytics, insight generation and social media and web monitoring. There is a clear increase in qualitative research as well, indicating possibly that the missing piece to make Big Data usable and smart is understanding the context and framing of questions, the why to analytics' *what* and *when*.

With continuing innovation, technological investment and new creative ways to generate customer insight, this growth is expected to endure while continuing to dramatically alter business models both within supply-side research organizations and the clients they serve.

Entering a second wave

Technology-driven change is not unique to research, and in the opening chapter John Gambles from Quadrangle reflects upon the impact of the second wave of digital and the effect upon demand-side with changing customer choice, loyalty and behaviour, and how this presents a perfect opportunity for enhancing research – but only if researchers adapt to bridge the gap, integrating research and data, and turning this into value for clients.

Nudge along

Ben Page from Ipsos MORI considers the fluctuating nature of public policy research: the different kinds of evidence being used to develop policy, how research is being deployed to evaluate the impact, and the wider inter-disciplinary skills needed by today's researcher to effectively leverage the new ways of thinking, particularly with dwindling research capacity within government.

Behavioural economics, exemplified by the UK Government's Behavioural Insights Team (or 'Nudge Unit'), has become a significant force in the development of public policy. Jonathan Fletcher and Dan Coffin from Illuminas reflect on wider applications within commercial research, setting out its relevance and value for health care research, plus some of the challenges such as the reliance on heuristics and the role of social influence and conformity bias among healthcare professionals.

Simon Shaw from Trinity McQueen explores the importance of context within behavioural economics, using two Royal Mail Market Reach case studies to understand how mail, leaflets and catalogues work as advertising media and the human problem of advertising misattribution. The case studies demonstrate the disparity between attitudes and behaviour using a mixture of ethnographic and neuroscience techniques including eye tracking, electroencephalography (EEG) and galvanic skin responses.

Pay attention

Andy Goll from Sparkler challenges the perceived wisdom that attention spans are reducing and demonstrates, with a Microsoft case study, that digital and mobile technology are actually evolving attention spans. Using reconceptualized lab tests as a fun and engaging game integrated into an online survey environment, and supported with some detailed observation of some participant's daily regimes, Sparkler developed attention-level personas with some suggestions for advertisers about engaging each group.

Culture clash

Cultural bias is almost completely impossible to eliminate, reports Conor Wilcock from B2B International, setting out how researchers can take account of it when undertaking research. He explores the specific issues that arise within business-to-business research, and the steps that can be taken to mitigate their impact, including adapting research language, methodology and response styles.

Lucy Morris from Spinach and Alexandra Wren and Mita Shaha from GSK tackle cultural challenges, reflecting on the value of using insight management techniques to help brands adapt their communications for better cultural impact, using a global case study for the dental hygiene product Sensodyne. The multi-market study covers a range of topics across emerging markets including the Philippines, Indonesia, India and China plus the developed markets of Australia, US and the UK.

People first

Behind all research are the people that contribute, the participants, and Maya Middlemiss from Saros reflects upon practical considerations when undertaking qualitative research recruitment, including some of the advantages and challenges of newer technology-based approaches. Maya demonstrates how recruitment can be undertaken, using a diet food case study, and includes some practical best-practice points to help those undertaking qualitative recruitment.

Janice Guy from Jungle Green reports on a project undertaken to assist Northern Railway to strengthen its rail partnerships, particularly among black and minority ethnic (BME) and socially excluded groups, discovering the power of a direct approach using Rail Community Ambassadors. This multi-award winning project set out to develop a blueprint for other organizations to use to engage BME and socially excluded groups, and includes 'People Stories' from those who benefited from the Ambassador approach by discovering the benefits of rail travel.

The heart of the matter

Central to all the chapters is people and their data – collecting it, using it, adapting it – and how this aids the development and understanding of business and society. To ensure that research continues to do this legally and ethically, Dr Michelle Goddard and Debrah Harding from MRS review the current data and privacy landscape, including the new European General Data Protection Regulation and its implications for research. Within this chapter wider ethical issues are considered, including the need to balance the social contract between researcher and participants, and the value of initiatives such as MRS's Fair Data trust mark in enabling businesses to go beyond their legal requirements, embracing the human at the heart of research.

Looking to the future

MRS aims to produce new Yearbooks annually. We hope you enjoy our first, and if you are interested in featuring in the future please do get in touch.

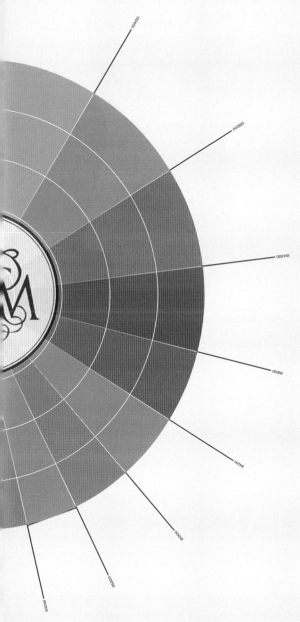

Special report: MRS at 70

The year 2016 marks the 70th anniversary of the Market Research Society. It's an opportunity to celebrate the social, commercial, creative and intellectual riches of the largest per capita research sector in the world.

For this special report, we asked some of the most influential names in the research business to write about their chosen game-changer – a person, technique or innovation that fundamentally changed the sector forever.

Images: Recent MRS data visualization with early MRS emblem inset

Photographs of Paul Bainsfair, Adam Phillips and Corinne Moy
© Will Amlot
willamlot.com

The birth of sentiment analysis

Adam Phillips

After World War II ended, it was widely assumed that Winston Churchill would be re-elected Prime Minister. So the landslide victory of the Labour Party was a shock. This was the first major failure of 'scientific' polling to predict an election result. The only research organization to forecast that the Labour Party would win was Mass-Observation.

At the time, this forecast was discounted because it was not based on a 'scientific sample'. Mass-Observation had synthesized information from a mixture of self-selected samples and qualitative work which included listening to conversations in public places.

In the case of the 1945 election, no one wanted to criticize Churchill publicly; however, conversations with friends were much more open, as people tried to find out if others were also thinking that Britain needed a change of leader. Mass-Observation believed that opinions not yet fully formed were inaccessible to traditional surveys until the person was close to voting. Diaries and overheard conversations among friends were likely to give a much better indication of the issues and the way undecided voters, or those influenced by social norms, were likely to vote.

Social media analysis and mobile ethnography are now accepted research techniques. What the Mass-Observers were hoping to create 70 years ago is now possible at an affordable cost. They were the first to develop the ideas that underlie sentiment analysis.

Adam Phillips is a Fellow of MRS and managing director of Real Research

The qual revolution

John Downham

Immediately after World War II, market research in Britain consisted of fairly straightforward usage and attitude surveys. By the 1950s, however, the emphasis had moved increasingly into developing the ability of research to explain, and not simply to describe. Attempts to uncover why consumers bought particular products and brands were given extra impetus by the growing concept of brand image.

In the middle of the 1950s came two potentially game-changing developments. One was the advent of computers into research agency work. Over time, this dramatically altered research activities, initially in the fields of media and panel research.

The second major development of the 1950s – the arrival of 'motivation research' – had more immediate effects. Up until this point, the application of psychological theory to market research in the UK had been limited and relatively uncommon. However, growing publicity for the work of US psychologists and psychoanalysts, such as Ernest Dichter, helped to increase interest – and heighten controversy – among UK researchers, advertising agencies and their clients.

The impact of motivation research triggered sometimes heated debates on a wide range of issues, including: How important is it for a survey sample to be representative of the survey population? And how is 'representative' best defined? What are the effects of interviewer–respondent interactions, and the setting and context of an interview? How can possible biases held by
the survey designer, interviewer or analyst best be allowed for?

Arguments about these and related questions risked creating a virtual polarization of the market research profession – qual v quant. It took some years for any general agreement to be reached about the appropriate relationship between the various research approaches. This upheaval, which started in the 1950s, can reasonably be described as a revolution – but it was one that led to a better understanding of the nature of differing methods and techniques, and to a more broadly based profession.

John Downham is a Fellow of MRS

Claus Moser and the LSE legacy

Geoffrey Roughton

Claus Moser, whose obituary appeared in early September 2015, received many tributes about the way he 'did so much to enrich Britain economically and culturally after the Second World War'. He was a polymath, a man of empathy and scholarship, a gifted pianist, a director of the Royal Opera House and a Master of an Oxford college, picking up a knighthood and peerage along the way.

In such a glittering life, Moser's contribution to our activities perhaps had less mention. But for market researchers, his 20-year tenure at the London School of Economics – where he became professor of social statistics – was seminal to the development of survey methodology. His subsequent appointment by Harold Wilson as Registrar General, meanwhile, helped to establish the value and independence of statistics.

For several years after 1945, LSE was pivotal in developing survey techniques. Claus was part of a hot-house of new ideas about social administration that brought him into contact with luminaries such as Mark Abrams, Maurice Kendall, Alan Stuart, Richard Titmuss, Peter Willmot and Michael Young. That decisions in this area should be evidence-based was an important tenet for Claus. His book *Survey Methods in Social Investigation* (1958) was a groundbreaking work and a very helpful reference at a time when many of us were learning these 'new' methods. Many of the methods we take for granted originated at the LSE; although the projects were social in nature, they spilled over into the commercial sector.

As Registrar General, Moser presided over some major changes: the General Household Survey and the Labour Force Survey are ongoing testaments to him. But perhaps the most important was to insist on the independence of the Government Statistical Service. He put his job on the line rather than agree to delaying the publication of a statistic that might have been inconvenient to the government of the day. That kind of intellectual independence has contributed to the ethos that underlies the principles on which contemporary market researchers hope to collect and present results.

Moser's comment 'Education costs money, but then so does ignorance' fits with his belief that good-quality statistics can educate policy-makers, and they should not be amenable to the whims of political masters.

Geoffrey Roughton is a Fellow of MRS and CEO of X-MR

The market research intelligentsia

Peter York

The market research intelligentsia was developed by people with a 'big picture' view, rather than a narrow, technique-based one; who were interested in the world outside the fortunes of the FMCG giants that dominated the client base when they had started working. They would be the people who would use, say, qualitative work for Heinz to develop big ideas about changing family structures, class variations in table manners and mass delusions about nutrition.

They were the first in the Sixties and Seventies to move out of the FMCG box and into political research, social policy research and working for charities. They were the first movers in relating qualitative and quantitative pictures of the world, leaving behind the nerdily partisan divide between the two approaches.

Conrad Jameson – a Harvard-educated American – was smart in every sense of the word. His offices, when I worked there in the 1970s, were in Belgravia, next door to Lord Lucan – just before all that. He was – still is – gregarious, talkative and hugely connected. By the time he hired me, his archive included various county council strategy initiatives, the Labour Party and a raft of design-led clients such as Sanderson. He believed research could drive social policies and design development because he was intensely interested in both.

Jameson taught me how to interweave qualitative and quantitative evidence for an argument (and how to make these arguments in 'mock mandarin' paragraphs that made Establishment-types sit up and listen). He taught me that the orthodoxy of 'validation' – doing a qualitative 'pilot' then validating it with some reassuring numbers – was completely wrong. You should, of course, do it the other way around.

Above all, he told me that market research, intelligently designed and persuasively reported, was the best basis for strategic thinking – miles better than the management consultants' MBA cookie-cutter analyses. So your client needs to have his hands on the strategic levers. Aim for the top and report to the CEO. When we started SRU, that was exactly what Dennis and I did.

Peter York is a Patron of MRS and a broadcaster and author

What I owe the geeks at IBM

Eric Salama

In the winter of 1982, I was busy writing my university dissertation. I used a word processor for the first time – some kind of precursor to the lovely Amstrad PCW 8256 that I bought a couple of years later – and I couldn't believe I could cut and paste, and correct errors without the use of Tippex!

Quite apart from the Sex Pistols and the Clash, the late 1970s and early 1980s ushered in two things – desktop computing and relationship databases. In 1977, the Apple II was among three personal computers launched on an unsuspecting public, followed, four years later, by the IBM PC. This computer was based on an open architecture that allowed third-party developers to flourish, and had 640KB of RAM and an audio cassette for external storage! People could use spreadsheets such as Lotus 1-2-3 and database software such as dBASE. Both became top-selling software products for years to come.

A decade earlier, Edgar Codd (be honest, have you heard of him?) was working at an IBM lab in San Jose, California, and was dissatisfied with the search capabilities in existing systems. This drove him to develop relationship databases and write the 1970 paper *A Relational Model of Data for Large Shared Data Banks*.

As the cost of computing has tumbled – and its power and storage capacity have increased exponentially – we have been able to undertake large-scale, global, quantitative survey work, and to analyse and interpret the results. As relational databases became the norm, we were able to look at individual-level attitudes and behaviour, and fuse data to understand cause and effect, and become more holistic in our analysis.

More recently, it has become possible to analyse gigantic amounts of census-level media, purchase and social data, and to use it to make our work more predictive and real-time – not to mention our ability to visualize data in ways that bring it to life and give it meaning.

I will always believe that human ingenuity, curiosity and creativity will continue to play a critical role in understanding why people behave the way they do.

However, none of us can underestimate the role that the geeks at IBM, Apple and elsewhere played in giving us the tools to transform our ability to capture and interpret data in meaningful ways – and in democratizing the process of market research, and opening it up to millions.

Eric Salama is CEO of Kantar Group

Geodemographics: the birth of Big Data

Peter Mouncey

I have attended most MRS conferences since the late 1970s, but a presentation that still sticks in my mind is the one given by Ken Baker, John Bermingham and Colin McDonald in 1979, introducing the first commercial application of geodemographics.*

The British Market Research Bureau (BMRB) team had been inspired by a lecture given by Richard Webber at the Centre for Environmental Studies in 1977, describing his pioneering development of a classification of residential neighbourhoods (CRN). This was shortly after BMRB had completely redesigned its main sampling frame using data from the 1971 census – what it believed to be the first nationwide computer-automated sampling frame in the UK market research sector.

Webber moved to CACI, and Acorn – the first full, commercial geodemographics process – was launched by the end of 1979, adding the codes to the full list of census variables.

Another important development at this time was the Royal Mail's introduction of a national postcode system for UK addresses, and its financial inducements to encourage database owners to add postcodes to their address records.

I believe this also led to the birth of Big Data, because – by using the postcode – geodemographic codes could also be added to each record. A whole new sector of marketing analytics was born.

Returning to 1979, the findings presented in BMRB's paper opened our eyes to a new world for marketers. As Baker described in his introduction to a reprint of the paper in two special issues of *JMR*s that celebrated MRS's 50th birthday, they enabled the 'Where should I?' question to be answered.

The indices presented by the authors provided a new view of consumer consumption patterns by residential area – whether it was for wine purchasing, credit card ownership, book buying or exposure to media. They also demonstrated its value to social research.

---

* 'The utility to market research of the classification of residential neighbourhoods', by Ken Baker, John Bermingham and Colin McDonald (BMRB), JMRS Vol 39 No 1, January 1997 – Proceedings of the MRS Conference, March 1979, Brighton

Since then, geodemographic coding – and the different systems – have become ubiquitous within market research and marketing. CACI and Experian (Webber developed its Mosaic system) remain two major players in this field, but there are several other companies providing such products – updated after the 2011 census – plus an open data ONS/UCL system.

Peter Mouncey is a Fellow of MRS and editor-in-chief of the International Journal of Market Research

Big data has changed our role

Corrine Moy

Since the turn of the century, there has been an explosion in the availability of data, both inside and outside client organizations – from CRM and transactional data through to point-of-sale data and radio frequency identification (RFID).

Meanwhile, the digitization of society has created hitherto undreamed of activities and concomitant behavioural traces – social media data, such as blogs, videos, photos; mobile and location data; digital behavioural data and e-commerce data.

Market research, of course, has long been an industry of data aggregators – combining surveys, but at the same time taking our clients' CRM and transactional data and making sense of this.

However, in the new paradigm that Big Data creates, our role has changed. We now need to define, for each customer assignment, what we measure and how. Traditional surveys are just one of the ways for consumers to make their voices heard – and given the wealth of data available via other sources, it is incumbent upon us to make surveys shorter and smarter.

Furthermore, market research is built around implicit and explicit consumer frameworks. By contrast, Big Data is unashamedly atheoretical. We, as researchers, have adopted a wider role – that of 'curators': identifying, sourcing, integrating, analysing and interpreting the full range of available data to deliver insights that we would not have achieved by more traditional means.

Arguably, we have become the keepers of the total customer view – not just for that bit of their day when they are visible to a brand. We can see the bigger picture by using all available sources to understand the holistic consumer journey and the motivations that drive it.

This enables us to combine our traditional currency of survey data with all forms of Big Data – to deliver truly 'smart data'.

Corrine Moy is a Fellow of MRS and global director of marketing sciences, GfK NOP

Smartphones as a measurement tool

Paul Bainsfair

The internet, particularly the mobile internet, has revolutionized the way people interact with media.

This creates many measurement challenges; however, one of the major reasons for this growing complexity – the smartphone – also offers the means to not only reach increasingly uncooperative respondents, but also to precisely monitor their actions.

A person's relationship with their mobile phone is incredibly personal. People, on average, use their phone every other minute.

Given that smartphones are with consumers throughout the whole day, they can be used in a variety of ways to interview respondents – from administering a standard questionnaire to asking interactive questions that are served after specific actions by the respondent, such as browsing a certain product or service, or entering a location. Not only can the respondent answer questions, they can also supply photos and videos of their situations, and take part in discussions – all of which are then transmitted back in real time.

Smartphones can also be used as monitoring devices; the total use in terms of calls, browsing, apps and location can be passively monitored via an easily downloaded app.

The use of smartphones as a measurement tool is a game changer and is growing rapidly as technological advances allow us to do more and more – for the most part, all relatively cost-effectively. However, we have to ensure we treat our smartphone respondents with respect, making sure we do not breach data privacy guidelines and ensuring that the respondent has given full permission to use their data.

We also need to make sure that we do not overload them with questions and that those questions do not become too intrusive. Last, but certainly not least, we need to make sure that we do not drain their batteries!

Paul Bainsfair is director general of the Institute of Practitioners in Advertising (IPA)

The launch of Twitter

Edwina Dunn

Accurately gathering information about consumers' needs and preferences no longer has to mean asking a question; it might include 'looking over a shoulder' online.

In less than a decade, 320m people worldwide have signed up to Twitter. Suddenly, the likes, dislikes, passions and opinions of a vast and diverse range of the global population are available publicly.

The connections people choose to make with influencers – such as brands, media and celebrities – unveil important information about them. And, since time on social media is given freely, these connections are a powerful window into how people live, or aspire to live. You are what you follow – what you're passionate about.

Customer data is a rich source of insight. What are they spending time watching or thinking about? What mix of interests do people display? What's in their digital shopping basket, across all their passions? Which communities do they belong to and how does this affect their transaction behaviour?

Traditional market research methods still have a major role to play in exploring these knowledge gaps, but what if you don't know which question to ask next, or which trend you should be watching out for? Analysis of Twitter behaviour – the whole audience, not just the vocal few – means consumers can now guide research, rather than the other way around.

There are 260m people using the social network who interact with five or more 'influencers'. This means – even if your customers aren't visiting or transacting often – they are still revealing important information about themselves elsewhere, all of the time. This is vital and transformational insight for the vast majority of retailers who record only one transaction a year.

In a world where consumers want brands to be timely, authentic and relevant, the insight from Twitter about your consumers and those of your competitors, all around the world – right now – cannot be underestimated.

Edwina Dunn is a Patron of MRS and CEO of Starcount

Digital, data and globalization

Sir Martin Sorrell

At WPP, what we once called market research or consumer insight is now described as data investment management (DIM).

Managing clients' investment in data – in a fragmented, complicated world – is what we do, just as we manage their investment in media (today we talk about media investment management rather than media planning and buying). These two areas are increasingly linked within our group, as we integrate data and media to provide clients with the most telling insights and the best return on their investment.

Some dislike the new terminology – and not only for the admittedly unfortunate abbreviation – because they believe it relegates the role of insight. Not so. Data collection and analysis is nothing unless it produces insights – and, as Jeremy Bullmore has so elegantly argued, insights have little value unless they are potently expressed.

Unearthing and communicating valuable insights remains the core purpose, and the traditional disciplines of market research remain very important in doing that. However, as digital technologies change the world, we need to be at the forefront of new developments.

One manifestation of this new reality is Kantar's pioneering partnership with Twitter to provide real-time social TV data, since expanded to new research products in the areas of advertising effectiveness, consumer insight, brand equity, customer satisfaction and media measurement.

So the web – and the data explosion it set off – have changed the game. But another force at work has arguably had just as much of an impact: the rise of fast-growth markets – the so-called BRICS, Next 11 and other nations whose economies have expanded so rapidly in recent decades.

Huge growth in the consuming classes has supported the development of advertising and marketing services and, within that, data investment management. The quantity of data and quality of insights now available to brands in these markets would have been unthinkable not long ago.

Millward Brown, for example, now produces in-depth BrandZ reports on the major brands globally and in China, Latin America, India and, most recently, Indonesia.

The digital/data/fast-growth market combination means, for the first time, we can offer clients a truly global view of consumer attitudes and behaviour – perhaps the greatest-ever opportunity for what we used to call market research.

Sir Martin Sorrell is a Patron of MRS and founder and CEO of WPP

The future

Honor Mallon

'There is a world market for maybe five computers,' confided IBM chairman Thomas Watson in 1943, while – almost four decades later – a young Bill Gates predicted that '640k of memory ought to be enough for anybody.'

Over the past 70 years, an avalanche of disruptive technology has transformed the research industry, so why should the future be any different? Can we predict what we cannot imagine?

Passive data is flooding our personal and business worlds: wearables measure our bodies; telematics control our cars; there are more mobile devices than people in the world, their numbers growing five-times faster than the human population.

As homes, wearables, vehicles and personal data exchanges become more connected, the devices will become smarter; shifting from reacting to predicting.

As our interactions with each other, our suppliers and customers, and the state increasingly take place via a device, the trillions of recorded daily interchanges become the new market research data. Recipients of insight will become blind to the sources of information, concerned only with their utility and ability to deliver competitive advantage.

If Big Data is today's disruptive revolution, our task is to find within it that which adds value to business decisions – a process of winnowing or sculpting rather than sampling; a new mindset of data selection, not just data collection. This means customers, employees and stakeholders will be connecting with researchers in a new context – and this is where behavioural economics, organizational psychology, ethnography, anthropology, and a host of other scientific frameworks for understanding people, can add value. If we can use these to pull practitioners out of those grooves, let's embrace it.

All of this will help break down the barrier between insight and action. Market research will no longer be things collected some weeks ago from a subset of people answering only the questions we thought to ask. It will be a constant interaction with the real world and in real time, helping us to better understand what is actually going on, to predict the impact of actions more fully, and to make improved business decisions.

As an industry we are the interface between business and the world. We will have to consider how we are organized to deal with the scale and speed of information.

Data visualization and storytelling are only a fraction of the future. Old measures of quality and rigour will have to be rewritten.

The relationship between research agency, insight department and business stakeholders will need to evolve. Creativity will come into data selection and not just data use. We will need to save time in the gathering phase so that we can spend more time driving value from the insight and deciding how to act. Businesses that neglect the new market research world will be forever stuck in their old grooves.

__Honor Mallon__ is a partner of PwC, research to insight (r2i) and she led a collaboration with MRS to evaluate the UK research market. A summary of the report starts on the next page.

Special report: The business of evidence

In this special report, PwC explains how disruption is driving change across traditional business models, and market research is no exception.

The 'business of evidence' market

From banking to media and insurance to publishing, disruption is challenging traditional business models and driving change – and market and social research is no exception.

From a £3bn market in 2012, that was looking to new ways to improve existing approaches, the UK's research market has exploded by over 60 per cent to almost £5bn, driven by data analytics, insight generation and social media and web-traffic monitoring.

The UK's 'business of evidence' market now employs around 73,000 FTEs, with close to 10 per cent of employees engaged in data analytics, where the market has grown by 350 per cent since 2012 and shows no sign whatsoever of slowing. Looking to the future, the sector is using innovative technologies to drive a new generation of customer insight where data from wearables, behavioural economics and social media listening will further expand a market already fertile with data flowing from the core traditional research methodologies.

Note: *Business of evidence is defined as 'the collection and interpretation of customer, citizen, or business information for the purpose of informing commercial and public policy decisions, improving management of customer or civic relationships, or improving commercial or public management efficiency'.*

The size and impact of the UK business of evidence market

When PwC's global centre of excellence for research and insight (r2i), undertook the original *Business of Evidence* research in 2012, commissioned by MRS, the £3bn UK market was already experimenting with technology and the early opportunities provided by data analytics. Then, it was clear that this was a rapidly changing market; but even PwC's confidence that the

The UK business of evidence market currently generates

£4.8bn

in gross value added (GVA)

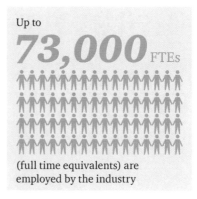

Up to

73,000 FTEs

(full time equivalents) are employed by the industry

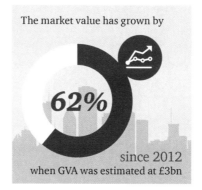

The market value has grown by

62%

since 2012 when GVA was estimated at £3bn

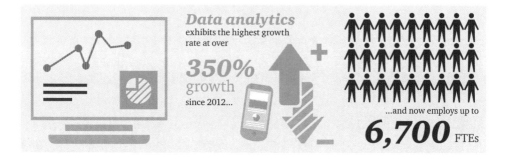

Data analytics exhibits the highest growth rate at over

350% growth since 2012...

...and now employs up to

6,700 FTEs

market would experience a dramatic technology-driven expansion could not have foreseen the impact of data analytics on the market.

Well over half of the participants in the *Business of Evidence 2016* research that were not market or social research organizations have in-house research functions, with data analytics and insight generation receiving the highest proportion of in-house research budgets. Looking to the future, 8-in-10 stated the volume of analytics they conduct will continue to increase, embracing mobile and other new technologies, while telephone surveys will go the way of the fixed landline.

Growth, decline and emerging markets

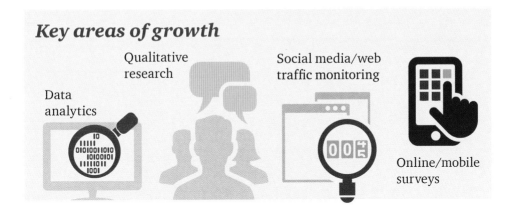

Key areas of growth

Data analytics

Qualitative research

Social media/web traffic monitoring

Online/mobile surveys

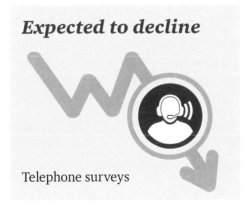

Expected to decline

Telephone surveys

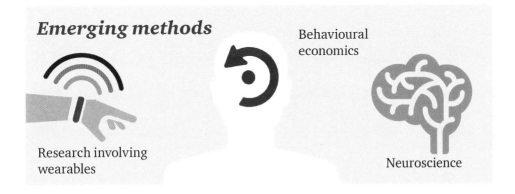

Emerging methods

Research involving wearables

Behavioural economics

Neuroscience

With a global analytics market currently valued at \$30bn, of which just under half (48 per cent) is customer analytics, there is little doubt that consumers will soon find that those who want to sell them goods and services will know at least as much about them, their lifestyles, their aspirations and even their bucket-lists, as they know about themselves. This is not a possibility for a distant point in the future, rather something which is growing right now and will continue to grow as more and more businesses begin to wake up to the ever-expanding treasure troves of consumer data on which they sit. With this backdrop, it is certainly unsurprising that those operating within market and social research and analytics, view the research sector to be a key influencer.

Views on the UK research market

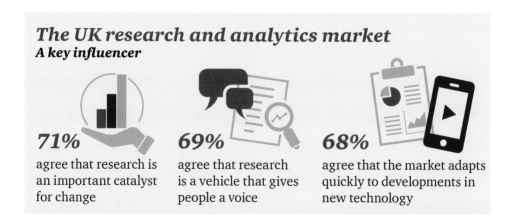

The UK research and analytics market
A key influencer

71% agree that research is an important catalyst for change

69% agree that research is a vehicle that gives people a voice

68% agree that the market adapts quickly to developments in new technology

Despite the dramatic growth in data analytics and the increasing ability to capture consumer data, the disruption of the research market should not come as any surprise. Last year, PwC's *Global CEO Survey* – acknowledged as the most comprehensive annual assessment of the hopes, fears and intentions of the world's business leaders – revealed that one in three (33 per cent) believed that a potential competitor to their business is emerging or could emerge from the technology industry.

As some of the world's biggest brands look for the next generation of growth, the natural response is to look to all of the demographic, financial and preference data for the millions of loyal, more transparent consumers –

what's not to like? Similarly in the B2B space, data on company performance, complaints volumes, open pricing or impact of social media sentiment on the brand, all provide immediate data points that are readily available and easily accessible.

There is, however, another area of growth in the market at the other end of the spectrum – that of qualitative research. Businesses can buy and mine big data at the drop of a hat, without as much need for primary telephone or online research. What is not as readily available is the ability to answer the why and the how? Understanding of behaviours, motivations and an anticipation of a consumer's next moves cannot be as easily extracted from data. The growth in qualitative research and more specialist techniques in this realm, such as ethnography, provide an important lens needed to understand and help interpret the data in order to deliver true insight.

If Big Data is today's disruptive revolution, then the research and insight providers' task is to find within it that which adds value to business decisions; a process of winnowing or sculpting rather than sampling; a new mind set of data selection and not just data collection. This means that people (customers, employees, stakeholders) will be connecting with researchers in a new context; and this is where behavioural economics, organizational psychology, ethnography, anthropology, and a host of other scientific frameworks for understanding people can really add value.

Unlocking the value of information – or not?

Harnessing the power of data and information that exists from all of these multiple sources brings us to another challenge facing the market and social research sector: unlocking the value of information to create insight and drive action. PwC has been asking organizations that commission market and/or social research what 'value' their spend delivers. We have found that there is a huge disparity across individual organizations between the best practice – where research is an investment that drives action resulting in improved business performance (ie value) – and the worst, where research can be seen as simply a cost burden.

PwC's Value of Research 2015 – PwC r2i survey of 184 C-Suite executives in the UK

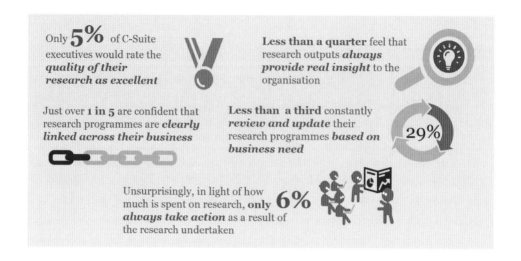

Only **5%** of C-Suite executives would rate the *quality of their research as excellent*

Less than a quarter feel that research outputs *always provide real insight* to the organisation

Just over **1 in 5** are confident that research programmes are *clearly linked across their business*

Less than a third constantly *review and update* their research programmes **based on business need**

29%

Unsurprisingly, in light of how much is spent on research, **only 6%** *always take action* as a result of the research undertaken

Using a figure of an almost £5bn UK market and social research market as a proxy for the amount that UK businesses spend in this space; one of our most staggering findings of our value of research study was that only 6 per cent of C-suite executives told us that they always take action as a result of the research undertaken. What are they using to drive strategy? And why spend valuable budget if you are not going to take action on the back of it? Organizations measure what they can measure (and have always measured) and this means they often miss the change that is all around them. Failing to research the future inevitably opens a door to inefficiency, disruptive technologies and new competitors.

It is not only this research deficit that is preventing organizations from harnessing the power of the information at their disposal. In a study recently published by PwC in conjunction with Iron Mountain, which investigates how companies are seizing the Information Advantage, three quarters of organizations told us that they were either constrained by legacy, culture and regulatory data issues or simply lack any understanding of the value held by their information. Furthermore, only 4 per cent of organizations have well-established information governance insight bodies, strong value realization cultures and allow secure access to those with the necessary skills. How can research, data and information make a valuable contribution in such an environment?

The real value delivered by insight

The benefits of strong research alongside powerful analytics is clear – increased efficiency, evidence-based decision making and reduced cost.

Top business benefits of research and analytics

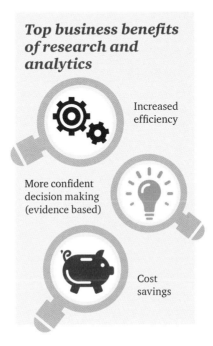

Top business benefits of research and analytics

Increased efficiency

More confident decision making (evidence based)

Cost savings

R2i believes there is an opportunity, if not a duty of care, to illustrate real value delivered by insight, to restore the reputation of market and social research and to promote best practice. This is about more than delivering data or populating scorecards, but actually about working with clients to use the data to drive business performance and make changes for better business. Just as the data landscape shifts, and established brands move out of their core markets and cause disruption, so too will the researcher of the future need to adapt and change.

The researcher of the future

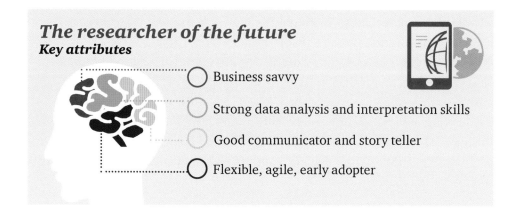

The researcher of the future
Key attributes

○ Business savvy

○ Strong data analysis and interpretation skills

○ Good communicator and story teller

○ Flexible, agile, early adopter

As we move from a culture of asking consumers what they think they might prefer, to analysing their consumption habits and recommending what they should consume, or from asking clients how they want to be managed, to investigating what their business really needs – the ability to get inside the mind and understand conscious and unconscious actions becomes paramount. Little wonder therefore that the ability to synthesize data from multiple sources and bring to bear business-savvy interpretation skills were deemed the two most important skills of the researcher of the future.

A mere 11 per cent of participants stated that a good grounding in traditional research skills was important for the researcher of the future – this is taken as a given, a hygiene factor and certainly no longer a differentiator.

So where does the new generation come from? A good question, according to the results of our market survey, where 61 per cent of participants told r2i that the research sector is an important incubator of skills, but over a third (36 per cent) also said they expect skills shortages in the future. Attracting and retaining key talent in the research industry is not without challenge, not just in the shape of the skillset but also in the shape of the image of our industry among future talent. The image of the traditional market and social research agency – one bound by rules, regulations and codes of conduct – should be seen not as one constrained by red tape but as one that creates ethical, innovative and insightful evidence which is used to inform business strategy and shape policy.

In conclusion

As a market, research is at the interface between business and the world. We will have to consider how we are best organized to deal with the scale and speed of information. Data visualization and storytelling are only a fraction of the future. Old measures of quality and rigour will have to be rewritten. Market and social research will be a constant interaction with the real world and in real time; helping us to better understand what is really going on, to predict the impact of actions more fully and therefore to make ever-improving business decisions. We will need to save time in the gathering phase so that we can spend more time driving value from the insight and deciding how to act.

Welcome to the brave new world of the *Business of Evidence 2016* – this world is changing and changing fast.

GVA and FTEs estimates by area

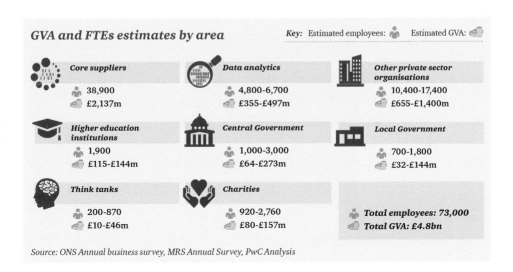

GVA and FTEs estimates by area

Key: Estimated employees: 　 Estimated GVA:

Core suppliers
38,900
£2,137m

Data analytics
4,800-6,700
£355-£497m

Other private sector organisations
10,400-17,400
£655-£1,400m

Higher education institutions
1,900
£115-£144m

Central Government
1,000-3,000
£64-£273m

Local Government
700-1,800
£32-£144m

Think tanks
200-870
£10-£46m

Charities
920-2,760
£80-£157m

Total employees: 73,000
Total GVA: £4.8bn

Source: ONS Annual business survey, MRS Annual Survey, PwC Analysis

The *Business of Evidence* 2012 and 2016 reports were commissioned by MRS and are available at www.pwc.co.uk/business-of-evidence-2016.html

Silicon Valley, Northern California.

◤ quadrangle

Customer know-how
in a digital world
_____

www.quadrangle.com

Tools for a digital world

01

We are in new times – the second wave of digital enhances the true value platform of research, explains John Gambles of Quadrangle.

Introduction: the first and second waves of digital

We started Quadrangle in 1987 and, for the first two-thirds of Quadrangle's life, our core business was strategic consulting. In autumn 2007, we shifted our centre of gravity away from consulting and moved into research to give clients the best of both worlds – a research skillset with a consulting mindset – under the banner of *Research for decision makers*. Since then, we've grown like topsy, picked up a terrific set of clients, are AURA's Agency of the Year and have won their Commercial Acumen Award three out of the five times it's been presented.

A few months before we launched *Research for decision makers* – on 29 June 2007, to be precise – the first iPhone went on sale in the US. This kick started the second wave of digital. The first wave of digital transformed the supply side across the global economy: over a quarter of a century, digital's first wave created whole new industries, changed all other industries and redefined what constitutes 'work' pretty much everywhere. Digital's second wave is now driving an equivalent transformation of the demand side, only faster. The second wave of digital is profoundly and irreversibly changing customer choice, behaviour and loyalty. People now do things, want things and leverage things as the norm that were impossible just a few years ago. What we're seeing is more than disruption. It's a permanent shift in market power to customers.

This has far-reaching implications for the research sector. Simultaneously, it exposes research's limitations and makes research more important. It opens up game-changing new ways to integrate research with data. Above all, the second wave of digital enhances the true value platform of research – yet it offers no guarantee that the research sector will benefit from this. That's because digital's second wave also brings with it new and different categories of competitive threat.

We are indeed in new times.

The value platform of research

For 20 years, Quadrangle's work centred on helping clients to create and implement customer-led strategies. By definition, that required us to understand our clients' customers: who they are, what they do and think and, crucially, what matters to them. We derived this from our own work with customers, along with client-held data and, particularly, the new research that we commissioned.

Our experience of commissioning and using research made us critical of the overall research sector. Our view was (and still is) that some research agencies (*a*) put too much emphasis on the process of research and inadequate emphasis on the purpose of research; and (*b*) are insufficiently concerned with what happens upstream and downstream of the research process itself. We concluded that, as a whole, many in the research sector do not understand – or sell – the true value platform of research.

The real value of research is not so much in what it delivers, ie information and insight, knowledge and understanding, vital though these things are; rather, the value of research is what it uniquely enables and makes possible. Put differently, the true value of research is latent, and is only realized through its application. Research has value precisely to the extent that it enables decision makers to do the other – in truth, more important – things they are concerned with: such as driving sales, building brands, satisfying customers, delivering performance and growing value.

The real value of research is as an enabler: research enables decision makers to create (and measure) customer and commercial value. Through its ability to do this, research can create enormous financial value for clients. That is the true value platform of research.

The two most important objectives for decision makers

Essentially, the value of research is rooted in its unmatched fitness for purpose as a tool that decision makers can use to achieve their two most important objectives. These are to create and deliver customer-perceived value, and to measure and improve business performance.

Research has a unique ability to help decision makers successfully achieve both of these objectives. That's why we describe research – particularly when combined with data – as *'the single most important tool available to management in the 21st century'*.

Before going any further, we need to unpack these two objectives to look at what sits within them. This is essential to understand the crucial role that research, along with data, plays in helping decision makers deliver against these objectives:

1. Create and deliver customer-perceived value

This covers customers, brands, products and services; markets, competitors, strategy and positioning; customer propositions, user experiences and customer service; narratives, marketing and communications; journeys, channels and touch points; innovation, NPD, R&D, testing and evaluation; consumer trends, cultural intelligence and future watching; etc.

As the list makes explicit, research is central to all of these. Research is uniquely brilliant at helping brands create and deliver customer-perceived value. That's because, in competitive markets, research enables decision makers to understand *what matters* to specific groups of current and potential customers, and to explore and test how to deliver *what matters* in ways that make money.

2. Measure and improve business performance

This covers both (*a*) customer-derived measures of performance such as satisfaction, experience and loyalty; usage and attitude; brand image and awareness etc, and, using transactional data, (*b*) commercial metrics such as sales, margins, retention, growth etc.

The 'measure' part is pretty straightforward: near-universally, research is used for (*a*), and data for (*b*). It's with the 'improve' part that things get more complex, since improving performance first requires an understanding of the relationship between (*a*) and (*b*), ie how customer measures relate to commercial metrics (and, though to a lesser extent, vice versa). Getting to this understanding is not straightforward and tends to require a good deal of iterative, analytics-based work over an extended period.

But the real power comes from then overlaying knowledge of what creates – and also what destroys – customer-perceived value onto this understanding. So, for example, if a client understands how movements in CEX measures translate into value (through for instance customer retention or spend), then research can be used to determine what drives these measures up and down.

Doing this creates a straight-line between customer understanding and value creation, giving decision makers an ability to directly impact customer value and to more accurately predict future outcomes. This is particularly powerful in helping clients with allocating resources (*Where will we have the most customer impact?*) and prioritizing investments (*Where will we get the greatest commercial return?*).

As the above suggests, research is brilliant at helping us understand *what matters* to people, and how we can influence this. Data are brilliant at allowing us to see *what happens* at any level of customer aggregation or disaggregation, and to put a hard value against this. But it is the combination of these that is unbeatable: using research and data together gives us the ability to impact *what results*.

The underlying model (and logic) is simple and compelling: understanding *what matters* enables us to target and change *what matters* and so improve *what results*. This model is shown in Figure 1.1.

FIGURE 1.1   The underlying model of research

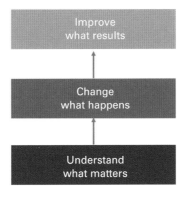

The uses of research

Unpacking the two objectives shows the near-total alignment between what sits within these objectives and what research, particularly when combined with data, is uniquely brilliant at. As this suggests, the two most important objectives for decision makers directly align with the two core uses of research.

The reason these are the two most important objectives is that they're about the two fundamentals in every business: customers and money. The first objective is about creating and keeping more customers, the second is about creating and keeping more money in the business. Ultimately, though, the two objectives meld into one. It's a simple equation: customers = money, because customers are where the money comes from. In the final analysis, that's why customers matter and why clients who are serious about creating customer-perceived value and/or improving business performance take a strong, near-obsessive interest in customers.

It is no coincidence that, together, the two objectives – ie to create and deliver customer-perceived value, and to measure and improve business performance – embody Theodore Levitt's great truth that the true purpose of a business is to create and keep a customer profitably.[1] It's no coincidence because, if research is about one thing, it's about enabling decision makers to do precisely that.

Similarly, it's no coincidence that the two objectives directly align with the two core uses of research. That's because, at root, the two objectives and two uses both reflect the transactional nature of a customer-oriented market system, where goods or services are exchanged in return for some form of value that is important to the performance of the business. Typically, this value takes the form of money but – particularly given the emergence of different business models linked to digital – it might also be customers, data, time or some other resource.

The two objectives and uses are shown in Figure 1.2.

As this figure suggests, there are two flows of value in a market system. The first flow is from the business to customers, and the second flow is from customers to the business.

FIGURE 1.2 The two key objectives for decision makers and the two core uses of research

Both flows contain tangible and intangible value. In the flow to the customer, the tangible value is the product or service that is bought, received and/or consumed. The intangible value is best articulated as everything that is implied by the notion of a brand, although it also embraces more functional attributes such as ease, timeliness and speed. In the flow to the business, the tangible value is the money (or data, etc) that flows, directly and indirectly, from customers. The intangible value is the kind of things that we track in research, eg satisfaction, reputation, advocacy, loyalty etc.

While there are complex inter-relationships between these four distinct categories of value, quite clearly both flows feed each other: the value received by customers drives the value received by the business – ie v2c drives v2b – while the value received by the business funds current and future value creation, for both customers and the business.

The uses of research are defined by this market system. That's because, allied with data, research enables decision makers not just to measure but to change the value that flows in a market system.

The second wave of digital

Any which way you cut it, the big thing that has happened in the nine years since we launched *Research for decision makers* is the impact that digital has had across the whole of the demand side. This is the second wave of digital.

The first wave of digital started in the mid-1970s and over a quarter of a century transformed the whole of the supply-side. This first wave created whole new industries, changed all other industries and re-shaped what constitutes 'work' pretty much everywhere. The first wave was driven by the Personal Computer, the second computing platform after mainframes. In the 25 years to 2002 over a billion PCs were sold, rising from about 48,000 in 1977 to about 125 million in 2001.

The launch of the iPhone in 2007 kickstarted the second wave of digital. Nine years on, we can see very clearly and very strongly how the second wave is having an equivalent transformational effect on the demand side. If anything, its impact is happening faster and more widely than the first wave. And, from what we already know about what's coming down the pipe, there's a good deal further to go.

Unlike the PC in the first wave of digital, what's at the heart of the second digital wave is not a single technology, though it sometimes is misread as that. Rather, it is the way that three distinct, though mutually enhancing platforms have come together since 2007 to create a new consumer reality:

- **The third computing platform:** The emergence of mobile as the 'third computing platform' (after mainframes and PCs) across a wide range of connectable – and, therefore, networkable – devices. The significance of this third platform is growing exponentially as both the capabilities built onto mobile platforms and the worldwide penetration of smart devices continue to increase rapidly. In under a decade, the demand side has become networked, with consumers able to connect to business – deciding who, when, where, how and on what basis – on their own terms.

- **Widespread availability of fast, high bandwidth connectivity**: This includes 4G and 5G; public and private wifi; home broadband and the apparently unlimited appetite among consumers for – at least the option of – being continuously connected. Ongoing improvements in speed, bandwidth/network capacity and what smart devices can do are feeding this appetite, and there is little, if any, reason to expect this to change until a saturation point is reached – however that may be defined.

- **The exponential growth of social media and other networking platforms across connected, often mobile, devices**: These networks are 'always on', enabling any number of people – 'friends', consumers, customers or, indeed, any variety of shared interest groups – to find each other, come together, to communicate and to discover, receive and share information of all kinds on connected, often mobile platforms in real-time. The speed at which consumers have not only absorbed these networks into their lives, but – in the case of rating sites such as TripAdvisor – have learned to leverage feedback for their own benefit is remarkable.

In its essence, the second wave of digital does three things. First, it **distributes technologies** that consumers value and can use, and which they easily, imperceptibly synthesize with – but then re-shape – how people live, work, play, communicate and consume. Secondly, it **empowers the demand side**, changing what customers know, think and do and creating new patterns of choice, behaviour and loyalty, in a way that is unprecedented. Finally, it **enables disruption** by new, technology-based players in a market, who are able to deliver a better value proposition.

The combination of these is game-changing for the supply side in a way that the first wave of digital never was. What we are seeing with the second wave goes beyond disruption – it's a permanent shift in market power to customers. Today, there is not a business on the planet that, at some level, isn't grappling with the question of how to succeed and make money in a consumer landscape that is being transformed by the second wave of digital. For a number of sectors and clients this is an existential threat, neatly if somewhat brutally summarized in a July 2015 *Forbes* magazine article that stated: 'If you're not a start-up, you're a turnaround'.[2]

The value of research in a digital world

All of this has far-reaching implications for research and the research sector.

The second wave of digital makes research more important while, simultaneously, exposing its limitations. It makes research more important for two reasons. First, and obviously, because digital's second wave shifts market power to the demand side, so there is now a greater and more urgent imperative to be – and stay – close to customers. The second reason is that this, in turn, puts a new premium on customer insight: the ability to continuously know and respond to what matters to customers is now a strategic asset.

Digital's second wave exposes research's limitations because, in a lot of cases, data are now able to better deliver the customer knowledge that, previously, clients had looked to research – primarily, though not exclusively, quantitative research – to give them. Data can answer the *who, when, where, how* and *how much* questions for different types of customers better than research because, at their best, data are faster, real time, comprehensive (census, not sample) and 'free'. However, it is not quite that straightforward.

For some time, data have given clients a good level of customer knowledge and understanding – think CRM, 'single customer view' and 'lifetime customer value'. What the second wave of digital does is to exponentially dial up the depth of customer knowledge, understanding and, importantly, insight that clients can get from data. This is because of the humungous and continuously expanding quantities of data of every imaginable type that digital's second wave generates from the demand side.

As described earlier, the real value of research is not so much in what it delivers, ie information and insight, knowledge and understanding, vital though these things are; rather, it is in what research uniquely enables and makes possible. Exactly the same is true of data. The challenge with 'big data' is precisely the same as with research: to turn what is generated through the data collection process – regardless of what this looks like – into something that decision makers can use to create and deliver customer-perceived value; and/or to measure and improve business performance. D H Lawrence wrote that, where some people see coal and some people see diamond, 'I see carbon.' The same is true of research and data, but here the carbon is insight.

Research and data *together*

Seeing the complementary – near symbiotic – relationship between research and data points the way to the future. Together, they are a far richer, more useful source of understanding and insight than either alone. Data give us the hard numbers to put against a research-derived understanding of people and their behaviours. Data are brilliant in answering the *who, what* and *how-much* questions relating to behaviour; but only research can get to the *why*. Data can allow us to profile, quantify and put a £ value on this behaviour, at any level of aggregation or disaggregation.

Research – and, particularly, qualitative research – enables us to explore, and explain the motivations, expectations, attitudes, value sets and beliefs that sit behind and drive people's behaviours; and, from this, to work out how we can best impact their future behaviour. Using research and data together in this way enables us to bridge from passively measuring performance, to actively improving it. From there, it becomes possible to develop both diagnostic and predictive business applications.

Commercially, this is breakthrough territory, since it gives decision makers the base information they need to prioritize efforts and investment so as to optimize ROI. So, for example, data allow us to see where growth is coming from, what the value is of different segments or who are the best customers; research enables us to engage the people who are the source of these data – individually, or as cohorts – so we not only understand, but can impact or action whatever is causing these numbers. Data allow us to see what (different) people do, and to measure the £-value of this; research enables us to explore and discover what these people think, feel, know, believe and value, so we not only understand why they do what they do but, crucially, gain insight into how we might influence them.

There are a couple of nice paradoxes sat at the heart of all this. First, one of the main ways in which the second wave of digital has made research more important relates to the exponential increase in the quantum of customer data that digital has driven. Of themselves, these data are interesting but not inherently useful; it's only when data become actionable, that they become truly valuable. And there's the first paradox: a primary reason digital's second wave has made research more important is that research transforms the value of all this data by making it *actionable*.

The second paradox comes directly out of the first. Precisely because of the humungous quantities of quantitative customer data that it generates, the second wave of digital makes qualitative research important. Or, more precisely, qualitative techniques, methods and approaches that help us not so much find out, as comprehend and make sense of things. Seen from this perspective, it is no coincidence that 'new' research methods like behavioural economics, neuro-science, semiotics, observation, self-curated content, etc. have grown in prominence alongside digital's second wave.

The fantastic thing about qualitative research is that it allows us to get behind the numbers, to peek inside people's heads and answer the why questions. To know *who*, *what*, *when*, *how* and *how much* in ever-greater detail is brilliant, and we are fortunate to live in a time when the ability to do that is increasing on a near-daily basis. But using qualitative research to answer the *why* questions raised by the numbers is awesome.

The future: integrated research and data

Simultaneously, digital's second wave makes research more important and exposes its inherent limitations. Data, though, more than compensates for these limitations, because of the depth of customer knowledge, understanding and insight that is latent in data. In this way, the unprecedented quantum of data generated by the second wave of digital significantly enhances the value platform of research. The challenge, as in research, is to realize the latent value of data in ways that make it useful to decision makers. That is very good news. It makes the value-creating – as opposed to data collecting – aspects of what we do that much more important to our clients.

However, and it is a very big however, there is no guarantee that clients will look to the research sector to do this.

The research sector has the skills and know-how to turn what is collected into insight; the data sector has the tools and expertise to create meaning out of data. The Achilles' heel of both is that, generally, this is where they stop. The bridge to usage – and, hence, value – is not built and the latent value of research and data remains latent. This is a space that the large management consultancies have spotted and, increasingly, look at with growing interest.

In the second wave of digital, whoever can integrate research and data, and turn this into value for clients has tremendous, unprecedented power. We believe this is the future and, over the last few years, have invested heavily in building a capability, expertise and track record in precisely this. Already, there are a significant number of 'integrated research and data' client stories we can tell and these are growing stronger all the time. We have brought all this together in a set of five core insight tools that clients need to succeed in a digital world.

We are in new times, and new times call for new tools. We call ours *Tools for a digital world*.

References

1   Theodore Levitt was the Edward W Carter Professor of Business
    Administration at Harvard Business School and Editor of *Harvard
    Business Review* during its most influential period. His most famous book is
    The Marketing Imagination (1984, revised 1986), which is, arguably, more
    powerful, original and important in today's digital world than ever before.
    He originally wrote 'The purpose of a business is to get and keep a customer,'
    though he subsequently qualified this by underlining the importance of doing
    so profitably. Along with Peter Drucker on management, and Kenichi Ohmae
    on strategy, he is among the most seminal of business writers. If you've not
    read him, you've missed a treat.

2   This phrase was brought to public prominence by the article in *Forbes*
    magazine by Nigel Morris, CEO of Dentsu Aegis, Americas and EMEA.
    However, it originates in Silicon Valley, as an article of faith in describing
    the disruptive impact of digital technologies. While a nice bit of hyperbole,
    it nonetheless embodies an important truth about digital's impact.

At Saros, we don't need

Our outreach programme has 50–150 UK consumers joining our database of potential research participants every 24 hours – not past participants, 'panellists' or survey-addicts, but over 300k genuine fresh members of the public, many of whom are registered preference service users and cannot be reached by other means.

This enables our talented Project Managers and in-house interviewer team to find exactly the respondents you need, to add that vital insightful contribution to your most demanding qualitative projects.

If your work deserves this please get in touch.

to bend people to fit

SAROS **Research recruitment re-invented**

www.sarosresearch.com/researcher

maya@sarosresearch.com

020 8481 7160

Widening access to qualitative research participation: giving everyone their say

02

Social media is helping us to improve both targeting and coverage in respondent selection when doing qualitative research, explains Maya Middlemiss of Saros.

In this chapter, we'll look at the craft of qualitative research, the challenges and changes within recruitment methodologies and the importance and benefits of widening participant access to research. This widening access approach means bringing in the broadest range of participants possible, and harnessing new technologies and techniques to achieve this. Working in this way not only improves the practice of research, it improves the potential for impact as well.

The craft of qualitative research

Understanding consumer behaviour

Qualitative research is selective, not representative. Exploring the perceptions, motivations and behaviours of small groups of people serves a very different purpose from the gathering of quantitative evidence, and generates a different kind of insight for our clients. The craft of the qualitative moderator is a joy to watch, conducting an individual or group interview as they gently and persistently get closer to the underlying perceptions and assumptions influencing consumer behaviour that the participants are barely aware of themselves, using a combination of direct questioning, projective techniques, creative exercises and group discussion.

The benefits of face-to-face vs online qualitative research

As a rule, qualitative research takes place using very small numbers of participants. While online tools have added a new dimension to the process, the probing that typifies qualitative research can only happen on a very direct and interpersonal basis, with an individual researcher reacting and pursuing a line of thought through with a small number of specific conversations. Online, the level of disclosure and reflection is hard to achieve, and the process could be compared to a quantitative interview or self-completion questionnaire. Techniques that involve the use of webcams and videoconferencing tools have brought greater qualitative depth to online approaches. But many researchers still maintain that it's easier to overlook nuances, body language and what is not said, compared with direct face-to-face conversation, where there is likely to be greater pacing and interaction between the researcher and the participant as two human beings – bringing all their conscious and unconscious communication assets to bear. Although a fleeting change of expression contradicting the words uttered might be captured on a webcam, and later reviewed, the likelihood of it being noticed and explored in the moment is simply greater when the two parties are face to face in real time.

There are of course many advantages to online qualitative research, such as being able to engage larger numbers, as well as including participants who would, for various reasons, including location, ability and availability, simply be unable to engage in qualitative research at all without the online tools now at our disposal. Practitioners are now able to choose from a very wide range of tools and services to decide which will best achieve their research objectives.

Defining the correct target for recruitment to qualitative research

Participants for qualitative research are selected because they represent a typology or segment that the researcher needs to explore, and have an attitude or behaviour that needs deeper understanding. They are not chosen to represent social segments or any kind of statistical sample of the population, as a rule. The selection criteria applied might include a range of behavioural, attitudinal and demographic conditions. But the former criteria will ensure they are unlikely to represent the demographic empirically, and often the demographic matching is for group dynamic reasons (such as a batch of six group discussions, divided by sex and also into three age bands, to facilitate group norming and flow).

The reason these people are defined and recruited for research is to represent the target which will best answer the questions underpinning the research objective. For example, questions such as:

- What motivates early adopters of products in this range?
- Why do we have significant lapsing users in the 35 to 45 category?
- How will the loyal clients respond to the proposed change in the brand image?
- What do core viewers of last year's series think about those two possible endings for this season finale?
- What is the reaction of competitor purchasers to our proposed new brand extension?

Qualitative recruitment specifications will define the sample to be recruited using a range of factors. These can be tested during recruitment using tools including questionnaires and telephone interviewing. These tools ensure that the participants selected meet all the correct behaviour and attitude requirements to contribute the material the researcher needs to generate actionable insight for their clients.

Ensuring the full range of opinions are represented

However, the largely unquestioned assumption within qualitative research is that in other respects the playing field is level: ie, that all consumers possessing such attitudes or behaviours have a likelihood of being present in a given focus group or depth interview sample. In other words, that the discrimination and selection take place on factors stated in the recruitment specification alone – all other factors being equal, any given demographic or segment of the community has an equal chance of being present in the group, so long as they are a female 25–35 lapsed user, or whatever is required.

Recruiting participants for qualitative research

Recruiter use of databases historically

In the past, many recruiters had extensive personal networks of contacts, often combined with formidable memories and that knack for making connections. Before technology offered anything that we would now recognize as a database, tools such as index cards and Rolodexes could be filled to bursting with useful information about potential participants and their particular interests and roles. Everybody working in fieldwork accepted as given that many projects would be filled this way, because the timelines involved in research recruitment simply didn't (and still don't) allow for going out on the street and finding fresh new participants every time. Besides this, how unproductive it is to find the perfect possible participant in this way and then to establish they were not free for the date of the session, or used the wrong brand of shampoo to fit the profile perfectly.

There were logistical difficulties with this traditional approach owing to the limited number of recruiters available, particularly in certain areas. The way that the industry evolved to outsource via freelance supervisors made it difficult to control who exactly was doing the work. However, before wide adoption of digital technologies within the research sector, this was a model serving the industry for the most part.

While recruiters did include some extremely tenacious and persistent connectors of the type identified above, social psychology indicates that we all associate with and most identify with people who are 'like us' in some way. Although any individual's network of personal acquaintances and relationships might appear highly diverse, it is more likely that you will meet in the first place – never mind form a meaningful connection with – somebody sharing at least some similarities with you, in terms of age, social background, ethnicity, attitudes, values and opinions.

There is no documented evidence of the impact of this on qualitative recruitment in previous decades, but the narrower the demographic pool of traditional recruiters in specific areas, the greater the likelihood of this affecting the composition of research recruitment.

Because good recruiters are sought-after assets, particularly in low penetration areas, it is not always easy to establish how projects are fully or partially outsourced. Nor are demographic profiles of qualitative participants monitored routinely – so, there is no way of telling whether any given focus group of say 10 women aged 25–35 loyalists of a specific shampoo brand actually reflects typical users of that brand drawn from the population of London or Glasgow or wherever the research is conducted. To do so would be unfeasible and for the most part irrelevant – if researchers insisted that out of that group at least three had to be non-white, at least one disabled, etc. Nor can it be stated with any accuracy how this would affect the outcomes, and whether the qualitative insights about the shampoo would generalize to the broader population likely to be purchasing it. However, if groups were consistently drawn from a restricted demographic, the potential for curtailed insight being drawn from an inappropriately narrow group is surely present.

The impact of technology on recruitment possibilities

In recent years, technological factors have combined to change this research landscape, starting around the turn of the new millennium.

Database technology

The first key impact of technology within qualitative research has been the advent of database technology, which has become flexible and affordable at small business level via standard software suites. This coincided with the first robust data protection legislation emerging in our market, the rise of Microsoft Office professional software and competitors that meant that suddenly more and more people had better ways to organize lists of participants and potential participants than any sorting through well-thumbed paper address books could accomplish.

New ways of collecting data

New ways of collecting that data in the first place quickly followed, as email tipped from being a minority business and academic tool to the ubiquitous phenomenon it now is. While there do remain audiences who are not, and sadly now may never be, digitally enabled, we have now certainly reached the point where for most projects this is not a relevant factor. In other words, we can safely assume that being able to respond to an email and complete an online expression of interest form will not be a barrier or distorting filter on the recruitment of participants. However, we do need to recognize that digitally excluded audiences include a range of groups, including older people

(32 per cent of people aged 65-plus are not digitally enabled, according to Ofcom), specific categories of disabled people and also those who are socially excluded for a variety of reasons (housing tenure, transient status and so on). Although there are government targets to reduce digital exclusion by 25 per cent annually, in 2013 it was identified that 7 per cent of the employed workforce had never been meaningfully active online – mostly lower socioeconomic groups, and there are also still parts of the UK that are very poorly served with high speed connections of any kind. Therefore the viability of each specific qualitative brief needs to be considered with regard to this.

Social networks

The internet and social networks mean that theoretically anybody can be exposed to a message about the potential to participate in qualitative research. It is also possible for anybody to set up tools to do this, and capture responses online. It is the interconnectedness of the online world which has truly changed participant recruitment for ever. It has changed how we discover, connect and communicate – in everything we do.

Social media can be a double-edged sword in many ways, and the sheer numbers involved mean that different approaches have to be employed. For example, one of the critical factors in qualitative screening is blind recruitment: not disclosing the 'correct' answers to screening questions, for reasons of both robust recruitment and commercial sensitivity. It is possible to see a number of examples of very poor practice, of far too much detail being posted of exactly what kind of person/behaviour is required in recruitment, making it impossible for fair and effective screening to subsequently take place.

It is possible, however, to use social media very effectively at the very top of the 'recruitment funnel', tapping into the social graph to target people who are likely to be a fit for any given project. But then they can be pulled into a full screening process involving online and telephone interviewing, against open questions, to determine actual fit for a specific qualitative project.

Recruiting the right participants for research through the online space

Identifying motivated respondents

Recruiting participants for research amidst the hype of the online world can be challenging. It is tempting for some to chase the lowest common denominator and lose their voice – and inevitably their credibility – amidst the general noise of 'get rich quick' promises.

It is actually far harder to capture attention by saying 'Don't get rich – earn potentially significant incentive payments by very occasionally taking part in research, and in the meantime trust us with lots of very personal information to enable us to find the right project for you.' Every recruitment company does need to collect contact information at the very least to build a participant database – like most others we collect far more than that, and it can be a long time before we find the perfect project for that person to take part in.

But the complexity of the recruitment message is a filter in itself. We know that we don't want people on our database whose sole interest is in earning a few pounds. They will have to work hard for their incentive money, possibly applying for multiple events before we succeed in screening them in, and then they will have to commit and travel to a research location and engage fully in the process, such as a group discussion. We therefore want to recruit people who are motivated to participate for the right reasons.

People are sometimes surprised to hear us say we have no interest in 'persuading' anyone to take part in research. Although of course some recruitment briefs are far more challenging to fulfil than others, in the final analysis every participant has to engage voluntarily and has a universal right under the MRS *Code of Conduct* to withdraw at any time – so we would far rather recruit somebody who is definitely keen and motivated in the first place.

Explaining the benefits of participation

The online space gives a real opportunity to educate and promote what being a qualitative research participant is all about, and why everybody – in our opinion – should get involved. This involves us, the recruiters, creating extensive content to explain that 'earning cash for your opinions' can mean something very different from earning a few pence or prize draw entry for filling in a survey.

We have to explain that it means taking part in a professional and well-organized event, where their interests, rights and identity are fully protected by a robust MRS *Code of Conduct*. They can expect to be listened to and consulted with, have their opinions perhaps gently challenged and probed by way of exploration, but respected and acknowledged in a dignified process. Their participation will not damage them, personally financially or professionally, and where they can share their views freely and confidentially.

It also means having a genuine opportunity to influence the way things develop, from marketing communications to technological devices and consumer goods. It is the chance to feedback to the brands they love (or hate); having opportunities to actually be paid for their ideas and opinions. It can mean even changing the way they think about how they make decisions as a consumer, how to look at everything from packaging to advertising.

These are the benefits that our participants feed back to us, about being part of qualitative research events, and this is what we strive to present to potential applicants, via on- and off-line communications across multiple media and platforms. The approach we prefer is to create a great showcase and shop window for the potential benefits of participation. We then invite people to come and register with us, to apply for specific events when they are ready, all of which puts them in control of the response and interaction wherever possible, to confirm their motivation and avoid pushy disruption.

Limitations of social media database driven recruitment

It is important to understand that database driven recruitment is not a solution to flawed research design, unrealistic expectations or badly planned field-work. It doesn't necessarily happen more quickly than traditional methods, because the process of interviewing and screening individuals still takes time. For traditional and database recruiters alike, it is the squeezing of timelines which has probably created the greatest pressure on research recruitment in recent years. Everyone wants their insight yesterday, and as communications and supply chain logistics have speeded up exponentially, clients want and expect that from research too. Those commissioning research can easily forget the fact that their potential participants have no stake in that urgency, no incentive for changing personal and professional plans to drop everything and go to a focus group tomorrow.

Social media can help us reach audiences of literally millions but it cannot do the job of screening and selecting participants for research projects. It can only act as the first point of entry to the recruitment process. Initial expressions of interest are only the opening stage of the process. When it comes to recruiting those who are the best fit for any given event, it still requires selecting participants who are also motivated, enthusiastic, opinionated, articulate and available – this all takes time, and qualitative judgement, which can only be supplied by a human interviewer.

Separating recruitment from selection

What the advent of truly database driven recruitment has enabled us to do is to separate the critical functions of finding people for research, from screening them into a given project. When recruiters faced the challenging task of doing both simultaneously, this process could be wasteful and stressful – and in the worst cases lead to pressure to cut corners on delivery. It is far more effective to devote specific resources to each activity. First, one stage that involves explaining and promoting and publicizing the role and benefits of being a research participant and another stage that involves recruiting and selecting participants to a particular brief.

The benefits and challenges of widening participation in qualitative research

Online recruitment widens access, but is not perfect

The combination of online data capture, the reach of social networks and digital communications, in general, have made a tremendous impact when it comes to widening access to participation. However, it would be dangerously complacent to consider the playing field effectively levelled already – that everyone can participate equally. The digitally excluded demographic may be reducing in number year-on-year, as many are among the oldest members of the community, but there will always be those who are not going to be reached with online tools.

One example of an excluded group is disabled people, who remain crucially underrepresented in qualitative research participation. The methodologies at every stage present many barriers, from awareness raising to screening techniques to accessibility of research venues, and this is before you even consider the barriers involved in effective participation itself. Outside the realm of specialist public sector and accessibility projects, we have recruited a great many people with varying degrees of disability to mainstream consumer qualitative research events, but often we have had to overcome complex logistical barriers as well as concerns and methodological challenges with the research itself.

At other times it has been a case of rethinking an approach altogether in order to enable equivalent and equally effective ways for participants to take part. For example, a deaf person requiring a sign language interpreter might find it challenging to keep up with a group discussion. Changing the approach, for example to an in-depth interview, could ensure participation and maximize an individual's contribution.

Widening access doesn't mean obsessive monitoring or even positive discrimination

When we are working on behalf of public sector funded organizations requiring specific quotas to be met, internally we prefer to avoid imposing targets and positive discrimination at the point of selection for given projects, in favour of working to ensure our database development materials are as diverse and accessible as possible. We know that the process is far from perfect, and it is something we are consciously working to improve, because it makes sound business sense for us to do so. Connecting with potential participants who are unfamiliar with research, and qualitative research in particular, and may have been previously excluded from research, means connecting with people who are fresh to the process and who can bring new ways of looking at things.

Wider access brings in more new participants

The commitment to widen access for research participation means we have to invest heavily in seeking out and registering hundreds of potential new participants every week, and for that reason deploying the digital tools at our disposal effectively is essential.

No doubt, it takes longer to conduct a recruitment screening interview with a 'virgin' participant, because there is more explanation and reassurance required, to make sure all concerns and reservations are addressed and the terms of engagement thoroughly understood. Although on the whole we are not out to persuade any diehard sceptics, people with little understanding of the industry have a number of valid questions about what will happen during the research session, how they will need to prepare, how the information will be used, how they will get paid and so on. We need to make sure they have a chance to talk through anything that is worrying them, and that can mean the interviewer listens hard for any understated concerns – because that concern can then turn into a potential cancellation or a no-show.

Sometimes it is beneficial to work with experienced participants

Some members of the Saros qualitative recruitment database have taken part in varying different events with us over the years, and have a better idea of what to expect. While we always try to prioritize the new people, we know that some participants have proved themselves genuine stars in different kinds of process, because of the unique way they think and come up with ideas – so we will try to reuse those talents where appropriate, and always after minimum rest periods and in completely different markets and activities.

Harnessing impact through qualitative research

Traditional qualitative fieldwork skills are still essential in the new world, and will always remain so. Arguably, as big data gets bigger and bigger, the softer and more human-based phenomena become more important as business decision drivers. They enhance the potential of qualitative research to truly have a strategic impact by bringing numbers to life with genuine insight and understanding, telling the stories that matter and shaping decision-making at every level. That understanding, of the research objectives and reasons for the exercise in the first place, has to be thoroughly embedded at the recruitment level, in order for the right participants to make it into the room.

Conclusion

Broadening the participant pool for qualitative research using all means possible is vital

Striving to widen access to the greatest possible pool of participant voices is vital to our trade. It is only by doing this that we can gather the fresh, unique, creative and original thoughts which enable our research clients to do their best work: generating actionable insights for their clients in every business marketplace.

Best-practice key points

- In choosing whether a qualitative recruitment brief is suited to database-driven recruitment, first consider carefully whether barriers of digital exclusion are likely to impact the representativeness of the selection.

- Always consider the participant perspective. What's in it for them? Does the project design offer them fair incentives, realistic lead times, a genuine experience of influence and a respectful and enjoyable interaction fully in line with the MRS *Code of Conduct*?

- Double-check all recruitment materials for inappropriate disclosure and leading inferences, which could undermine the blind recruitment standard or violate the client's intellectual property. Bear in mind that the message may get shared and forwarded way beyond the initially intended audience.

- Never lose sight of the fact that in qualitative research particularly, recruiters often represent the public face of the industry. They might screen 300 people, to recruit the eight who make the group discussion – and the impression they make is proportionately responsible for wider public perceptions.

CASE STUDY   Diet food product

The producer of a new low-calorie food replacement product needed to test their marketing communications with potential customers in their target market – in this case significantly overweight people (Class 2-plus obesity). It was a product which could be used as a total diet for supervised dramatic weight loss or more flexibly on an intermittent basis. Hence it had to appeal to people with varying levels of need.

This was a sensitive and challenging area that would be difficult to imagine tackling by traditional on-street recruitment methods. However, a screening process was devised which included:

- A sensitively and carefully-worded invitation to people in the demographic target.

- An online screening process that addressed:

  - weight, height and dress size (a valuable sense-check as BMI does not always tell the full story);

- history and attitudes to weight loss and health concerns;
- careful screening against any history of disordered eating and related psychiatric or other medical conditions.

• Sensitive and probing telephone interviewing by trained research bookers, exploring participants' comfort levels in talking about their relationships with food and dieting with strangers, their willingness to self-disclose and talk about previous attempts to lose weight, as well as their perceptions of the weight loss industry and marketing messages.

• Very carefully planned and worded messages for potential participants who ultimately screened out and were not selected for the face-to-face paid element of the research. We needed to recognize that when sensitive disclosure is required in screening, participants make themselves vulnerable in a way they do not when answering a questionnaire about brands of shampoo. It was vital in particular that nobody felt rejected from the process for reasons of weight, as this was a criteria upon which they frequently felt judged in their everyday lives.

A decision was made to divide the sessions into a larger number of smaller sessions, grouping participants by body mass index. During screening it emerged that extremely overweight people felt very self-conscious about discussing weight issues with people they regarded as having less serious or challenging targets. Conversely, those looking to lose a stone or two for the summer were inhibited by the idea of voicing their minor concerns around people with major life-threatening weight issues, and they obviously required very different language and approaches with regard to brand positioning.

This was an excellent example of how selecting a database-driven approach in combination with listening to the finding during recruitment it was possible to create a 'safe' and dignified process for some very non-typical research participants to come together and share their opinions. This not only helped a brand shape the campaign for their new project but also provided a research experience that was described very positively by those who took part.

We are trusted partners to the world's leading brands

We have only two stakeholders — you and us

We are Illuminas

We are a full service consumer and B2B research agency and for 25 years we've been developing the best research practitioners in their fields.

We are an independent partnership led by researchers with no external shareholders.

We are method neutral, data neutral and develop custom research solutions that help brands make informed decisions to fuel growth and leadership.

We only consider a job to be finished when our client is happy; our track record of industry awards and long-standing client relationships suggests that we get it right most of the time.

 Illuminas

illuminas.com

Using behavioural economics in healthcare research

03

The high profile of behavioural economics (BE) in recent years has led to renewed focus on the non-rational, unconscious nature of everyday decision-making, explain Jonathan Fletcher and Dan Coffin of Illuminas.

This chapter shows the relevance and value of a BE approach to research in a professional area of decision-making which is often thought of as highly rational and evidence-based: prescribing practice. It starts by looking at the basic assumptions and principles of BE. We then introduce an approach which integrates research and BE that we have called Exploratory Behavioural Economics. Using published studies and our own experience of research in the healthcare sector, it shows that prescribing decisions are often based on the types of non-rational and unconscious mechanisms that BE identifies and looks at why this is the case.

The challenge of behavioural economics

According to the view of behavioural economics most of our regular decisions are characterized by six features:

1 They rely on heuristics – time- and energy-saving shortcuts or rules of thumb that simplify and speed up decision-making.

2 These shortcuts rely heavily on *sensory cues* – a highly selective subset of the total amount of information that is potentially available for making a decision.

3   The selection and use of these heuristics and cues occurs at an unconscious level. Generally speaking, people have very limited insight into their own unconscious processes.

4   The processes are subject to a range of *emotional biases* which may result in non-rational or even apparently irrational decisions.

5   Decisions made like this are very sensitive to the context in which the decision is made, including factors which might appear to be entirely extraneous.

6   When making decisions in this way we settle for solutions which are 'good enough' rather than seeking 'best possible' outcomes. This is known in the BE jargon as 'satisficing'.

We usually have to make our everyday decisions in situations where time is limited, where there is imperfect information, where considerations are hard to compare directly and where complete certainty about outcomes is not possible (where there is always room for doubt). The more that these circumstances apply when we are making a decision, the more likely it is that our decision will exhibit the six features listed above.

Although we generally lack direct access to our own unconscious, emotional reasoning processes, we do have a strong tendency to post-rationalize our behaviour. When asked why we have acted in a particular way, we tend to answer so as to present ourselves in a positive light, as having made a decision for rational, selfless motives which conform either to whatever social norms we think apply to this type of decision or which fit with our ideal self-image (or at least a self-image which we find comforting and acceptable). Sociologist Charles Tilly has written an entire book[1] describing the various objectives we have when giving reasons for our behaviour; giving an honest, accurate account of our motives does not get a mention!

This clearly presents a *challenge to research*: how can we get around the tendency people have to post-rationalize their actions to uncover the unconscious contextual and motivational causes underlying their decisions?

Exploratory behavioural economics: the marriage of BE and MR

Behavioural economics is often associated with methods which address this challenge by focusing on behaviour in tightly controlled, experimental set-ups.

These approaches result in concrete, clearly-defined contributions to the overall body of knowledge about their subject matter. But they are limited in the extent to which they can build an integrated understanding of the motivations and processes underlying particular decisions. And it is this understanding of the hidden machinery of decision-making that is needed in order to generate improved policies, products and services, communications and packaging etc. This requires what we might call *exploratory behavioural economics*: a blend of BE and market research, each influencing and benefiting the other.

The main contribution of market research to this partnership is the range of methods developed by researchers for getting beyond post-rationalized responses and accessing the unconscious causes of behaviour. These include:

- establishing the context in which the decisions are actually made; identifying those features of the context which influence the decisions;

- focusing on actual behaviour; observations made or recorded in real time or as close to real time as possible;

- encouraging responses which are not consciously mediated, such as projective exercises, visual stimulus materials and gamifying techniques;

- using 'distract and derive' methodologies; quantitative approaches which combine question set-ups to suspend participants' rationalizing tendencies with analysis methods which measure underlying, unconscious values. They include derived importance methods, choice-based conjoint analysis and implicit association tests (IATs);

- counter-bias questioning techniques. Framing questions so as to counter a known bias.

The main contribution of BE to the partnership is the range of heuristics and biases it has identified that affect decision-making. A key early stage in exploratory behavioural economics is to develop hypotheses from the literature to test in the data collection stage. This process starts with a review of what is already known or can reasonably be inferred about the decision-making task we're researching. Then we identify the range of unconscious decision-making mechanisms which could potentially affect this type of decision, and develop explicit hypotheses and lines of enquiry about the role which these mechanisms might play.

There is a set of contextual influences, constraints and incentives that should be considered when preparing to research any type of real-world decision.

The following questions should be reflected on at the outset of any exploratory behavioural economics study:

- **Risks and rewards**: What does the decision-maker believe they stand to gain from getting this decision right and what might they lose if they get it wrong?
- **Outcome sensitivity**: What would count as getting the decision right in the mind of the decision-maker?
- **Complexity**: How difficult is it to make this decision? How many factors should be considered and how much information is available?
- **Uncertainty**: What types of uncertainty might affect this decision?
- **Time pressure**: How much time is available to make this decision?
- **Social influences**: What social pressures, either conscious or unconscious, direct or indirect, is the decision-maker under?

Figure 3.1 summarizes the initial stages of an exploratory behavioural economics study.

The last line of enquiry in the data collection stage is to ask participants why they behaved or decided as they did. Encouraging participants to give their reasons for what they did, allowing their post-rationalizing tendencies full rein, is important to a comprehensive understanding of most decisions. There is a risk, when focusing on causes that the decision-maker is largely unconscious of, that you overlook the importance of what *they believe they are doing*. A decision-maker may be brought to the threshold of a decision by unconscious or suppressed causes, but may still seek conscious justification to cross the line and make the decision.

Analysis and interpretation

Generating hypotheses at the start of a study could lead to the psychological trap of looking only for information that supports your theory. The safeguards against this risk will, again, be familiar to most researchers.

In quantitative analysis, significance tests can be used to guard against these errors. If the difference on a variable between a control and experimental group is not large enough, you must reject your causal hypothesis. If a regression analysis accounts for only a small percentage of the variance in a dependent variable, then you know that something was missing from the list of variables you hypothesized as being important causes of a particular behaviour.

FIGURE 3.1 Exploratory Behavioural Economics: the initial stages

PREPARATORY STAGE

Review what is known or can reasonably be inferred about **the decision-making task**

Identify likely **contextual influences** on the decision-maker:
- Risks and Rewards
- Outcome sensitivity
- Complexity
- Uncertainty
- Time pressure
- Social influences

Identify the **range of psychological mechanisms** (biases and heuristics) which **might play a role in** the decision

Develop explicit **hypotheses and lines of enquiry** about the role which these mechanisms might play, for **testing in the interview/ observation**

DATA COLLECTION STAGE

Establish the decision-making context
- Using observation at the site of the decision.
- With direct questions about likely causes of behaviour.

Focus on actual behaviour
Observed and / or recorded in real time, or close to real time / asked in a non-evaluative way, early in the interview.

Elicit descriptions of processes
Get as much about the causes of their behaviour as is available to participants through conscious introspection.

Encourage responses which are not consciously mediated
- Projectives, Visual Stimulus
- Gamification

Use Distract-and-Derive techniques
- Drivers analysis
- Choice-Based Conjoint analysis, Implicit Association Tests

Use counter-bias questioning techniques
eg 'Permission-giving' - frame questions so as to make participants comfortable admitting to motives they may feel inhibited about sharing.

Ask 'Why?'
Encourage participants to give their reasons for what they did – allowing their post-rationalization tendencies full rein.

FIGURE 3.2   Causes and reasons

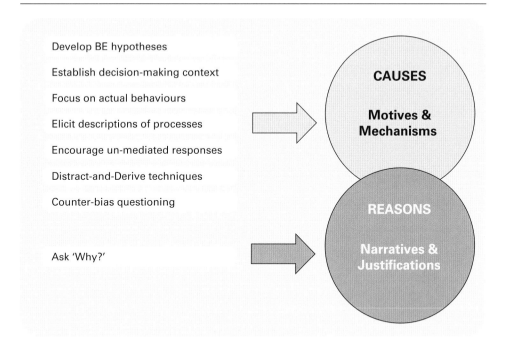

In qualitative research the following measures should be taken to guard against the risk of narrow theorizing:

- Generate a number of different hypotheses at the outset.
- Try to find hypotheses to test that are mutually exclusive or at least in tension with one another.
- Remain open to the possibility that any given hypothesis could be wrong.
- Involve a number of researchers in the analysis and interpretation.
- If you can't decide between two or more hypothesized causes for a behaviour, report on all of them. Then to weight them, or decide between them, either conduct quantitative research or compare the different practical considerations attached to putting each of them into action.

Behavioural economics in healthcare

Having outlined what is involved in exploratory behavioural economics, we now turn to the issue of its relevance and application to healthcare research. We will look at the features of prescribing decisions which make behavioural economics a natural approach in the healthcare field and some of the specific heuristics and biases which result from these features.

Prescription under uncertainty

The less certain we are about the outcomes of a decision, the more likely we are to use simplifying heuristics. The main source of uncertainty when prescribing is the likely response of a patient to a particular treatment. Just as patients differ in the symptoms they exhibit, so patients respond differently to treatments. Figure 3.3 shows exactly how common it is for a drug not to work for some patients even though it has worked for others.[2]

The more uncertainty there is from either of these two sources, the more likely a prescriber is to rely on heuristics to arrive at a treatment decision.

FIGURE 3.3   One drug to cure them all? Percentage of patients for which a particular drug in a class is ineffective

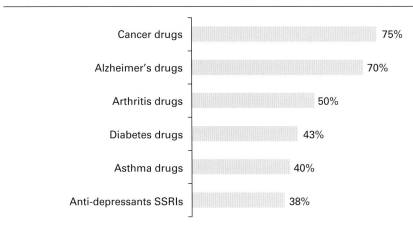

Cancer drugs	75%
Alzheimer's drugs	70%
Arthritis drugs	50%
Diabetes drugs	43%
Asthma drugs	40%
Anti-depressants SSRIs	38%

SOURCE: Spear, Heath-Chiozzi and Huff, 2001.

The high cost of time and cognitive effort

The less time we have to make a decision the more likely we are to simplify decisions by using heuristics (ie shortcuts or rules of thumb). And the time available to healthcare practitioners for diagnosing and prescribing treatment for each patient is very short. The Royal College of General Practitioners estimates that the average number of consultations carried out per year by a GP in England is about 11,000.[3] This equates to an average of about 60 patient contacts per GP, per day, and an average appointment length of about 10 to 15 minutes. Half of specialist consultants in the NHS feel they are 'always' or 'often' under excessive pressure. Only 12 per cent feel they are 'rarely' or 'never' under excessive pressure.[4] Reliance on heuristics under such conditions is almost inevitable.

Research into what psychologists call 'cognitive fluency' has shown that information of a kind or in a domain that we are not fully familiar with requires greater cognitive effort to process than information of types or in domains that we are fully conversant with. We have found that the wider the range of conditions that healthcare practitioners deal with, the more likely they are to use simplifying heuristics when prescribing for a particular condition, especially those conditions that are outside what they consider to be their core area of competence.

There is considerable evidence of reliance on a range of simplifying heuristics in the decision-making processes of healthcare practitioners.

Heuristics and norms on prescription

One of the most common heuristics used by prescribers that we find in our research is trial and error. The trial and error approach involves making repeated, varied attempts until a satisfactory outcome is achieved. It tends to be deployed where definitive knowledge is lacking and typically attempts to find an *acceptable* solution, not necessarily the *best* one.

Trial and error works well in chronic diseases with obvious symptoms and where response to treatment is reasonably quick. But it is less useful in acute illnesses, in diseases that produce no clinically obvious symptoms (so-called 'silent diseases') or in diseases where response to treatment is slow or outcomes are delayed. In these situations, second-hand empirical evidence is needed to compensate for the absence of the direct feedback used by the trial and error heuristic to determine effectiveness. This usually takes the form of data from clinical trials or statistics about outcomes from use by other prescribers.

The trial and error approach sets a high standard for subjective confidence. And when prescribers have to use a substitute indicator of therapeutic efficacy, credibility can become a problem. A study into the adoption of beta-blockers to reduce mortality rates after myocardial infarction (heart attack) showed that one of the key factors determining whether beta-blockers were being used was the provision of clinical evidence of the effectiveness of the treatment and that the credibility of this evidence was key.[5]

In a large-scale US study of therapeutic practices in depression and other chronic conditions,[6] researchers found extensive use of heuristics centred on 'norms': the prescribing of a small group of drugs (sometimes only one) to all patients with a particular condition. The authors concluded that in most cases these heuristics were probably optimal in light of the time limitations on consultations and the ability of practitioners to gather and process information about the patient's condition. But they also found evidence that, in a small but significant proportion of consultations, physicians appeared to be making prescription decisions that completely ignored or drastically over-simplified the differences between patients' conditions.

The 'familiarity' principle and the 'similarity' heuristic

All other things being equal, we tend to prefer things with which we are familiar to those with which we are less familiar. Successful marketing of a new product, especially in risk-averse contexts, often succeeds not by differentiating the product from existing products in the market, but by positioning it as 'the same but better'. Medical practice, while it may be open to the idea of new treatments, nevertheless has to focus on each individual patient. Practitioners cannot risk sacrificing the interests of the patient for the sake of advancing medical knowledge in general. This combination of a commitment to long-term progress with concerns about the immediate interests of the patient makes reliance on the similarity heuristic quite likely.

This has implications for companies when they are introducing new drugs. When a new treatment is communicated to practitioners, what is new about it can get filtered out. Instead of making room for the new concept in their existing understanding, practitioners may unconsciously alter the concept to fit with their existing knowledge in that area. (In the language of psychologists, instead of accommodating their current schemas to the new concept, they assimilate the concept to the schemas.) This can be a particular problem for treatments where the benefit, though significant, is not immediately obvious but only emerges in the longer-term.

The role of social influence and conformity bias

Professional and in-role pressures combine to influence practitioners to conform to perceived best practice among peers. To take a position that differs from the consensus is risky: even if you're wrong, there's a certain safety in numbers. And this is even true in medicine. Another finding of the study on beta-blocker adoption was that besides data on clinical effectiveness, physicians also wanted to see data which showed that other physicians were using beta-blockers. They wanted the reassurance that their peers in their own or other hospitals were using the new treatment. In similar vein, a study on the adoption of new antipsychotic drugs found that prescribers working in solo practices were slower to adopt the new drugs than those working in group settings, such as group practices or hospitals.[7]

Availability bias

The availability bias is the tendency to attach more importance to factors which we find it easier to bring to mind. This bias can be a major factor in decision-making in frontline medical practice.

In the study of prescribing practices in depression, it was found that a doctor's prescriptions reflected the severity of the conditions they were presented with, but showed no evidence of responding to the worsening of a patient's condition between appointments. Their decisions were being based on the immediate evidence in front of them rather than taking into account the next layer of information which would be a little less available, requiring as it did additional communication with the patient or referral to notes on the previous consultation.

There is clearly an awareness within the healthcare sector that the time-pressured and cognitively demanding environments in which they work makes practitioners prone to the availability bias. Participants in the beta-blocker study identified the need for a range of reminders of the importance of beta-blockers to ensure that the option was not overlooked. Hospitals in the study used a range of ways to reinforce the reminder. These included chart and poster-based reminders, embedding beta-blockers in treatment pathways and protocols and incorporating the drug into discharge procedures, right through to hiring care co-ordinators to remind doctors of their benefits and provide feedback on how much they were using them.

We find that healthcare professionals often value visits from sales reps from pharmaceutical companies precisely because they provide a form of reminder about a particular drug. These visits are part of the mental props which healthcare practitioners use to overcome the challenge presented by availability bias.

When is a behavioural economics approach indicated?

Aspects of the behavioural economics approach can be applied to a wide range of research projects. It is particularly useful in situations where there is debate about the likely pace of future change in a market. The biases and heuristics are fairly ancient habits of mind and tend to adapt only slowly and with considerable encouragement to new practices, products and services.

BE is also very helpful in understanding cases where buyers or consumers appear to be behaving in unexpected, irrational ways, or in ways that do not serve their best interests. In addition to this, it is of value in situations where the motives and processes underlying decisions are likely to be unconscious, either because they are made very quickly in absolute terms or because, as in healthcare, they have to be made quickly relative to the amount and complexity of information that has to be processed.

References

1   Tilly, C (2008) *Why? What happens when people give reasons... and why?* Princeton University Press

2   Spear, B, Margo Heath-Chiozzi, M, Huff, J (2001) *Clinical Trends in Molecular Medicine*, Volume 7, Issue 5, 1 May, 201–204

3   '34m patients will fail to get appointment with a GP in 2014'. Royal College of General Practitioners www.rcgp.org.uk/news/2014/february/34m-patients-will-fail-to-get-appointment-with-a-gp-in-2014.aspx Publication date: 23 February 2014. Retrieved 18.3.16

4 Census of Consultant Physicians and Higher Specialty Trainees in the UK, 2014–2015. Royal College of Physicians, Edinburgh, and Royal College of Physicians and Surgeons of Glasgow

5 Bradley, E, Holmboe, ES, Mattera, JA, Roumanis, SA, Radford, MJ and Krumholz, HM (2001) A qualitative study of increasing beta-blocker use after myocardial infarction: Why do some hospitals succeed? *Journal of the American Medical Association*. May 23–30 , 285 (20): 2604–11

6 Frank, RG and Zeckhauser, RJ (2007) Custom-made versus ready-to-wear treatments: Behavioural propensities in physicians' choice. *Journal of Health Economics* 26, 1101–1127

7 Huskamp, H, O'Malley, AJ, Horvitz-Lennon, M, Taub, AL, Berndt, E, Donohue, J (2013) How quickly do physicians adopt new drugs? The case of second-generation antipsychotics. *Psychiatric Services* April 1, 64(4): 324–330

Insight management

04

U sing insight management techniques can help brands adapt their communications for better cultural impact, explain Lucy Morris (MD Spinach), Alexandra Wren (Global Insights Director GSK Consumer Healthcare) and Mita Shaha (Global Insights Manager GSK Consumer Healthcare).

Adapting communications

Global brands are always looking for ways to achieve strong communications impact across markets but this can't always be achieved by rolling out the same messages or creative approach across vastly different countries or regions. The Sensodyne brand team faced this challenge. Together with their partner, advertising agency Grey, they recognized that they could achieve greater persuasion with consumers in key emerging markets by adapting their communications. They looked closely at cultural attitudes and behaviours to achieve a level of understanding to make this possible. After validating their findings and strategy in some initial emerging markets (Philippines and Indonesia), they started to apply the same intention to other emerging markets (India and China) as well as extending it to developed markets too (Australia, UK and USA). It was the use of insight management techniques and effective collaboration behaviours that enabled the local nuanced insights to emerge and get channelled into more effective communications. In this chapter we explain how this was done.

CASE STUDY   Sensodyne – culturally adapting communications for impact

Introduction

The Sensodyne brand has a highly effective advertising approach, which is expert-led across media and applied consistently around the world. However, as the sensitivity oral care category grows increasingly competitive, it became clear that the messaging and tonality would benefit further from an injection of consumer-relevant insight and that this needed to be sharp and culturally nuanced in order to improve the crafting and impact of communications. Figure 4.1 shows the traditional approach taken in the Indonesian territory as an example.

Global insight investigations

To fulfil the brief, the Global Sensodyne insight team within GlaxoSmithKline (GSK Consumer Healthcare), working with Spinach and advertising agency Grey, initiated a series of different market investigations with the aim of identifying insights that could lead to sensitivity treatment persuasion in each market. Each market investigation entailed a review of existing data, drawing upon trend intelligence, and then filling any gaps in consumer insight with qualitative research or online panel work. The need to develop culturally nuanced communications in several markets rapidly led to the development of a tailored four-stage insight programme, internally branded *Ignite*, that the global brand team could delegate to individual market teams to run.

The aim within each market

The aim of each market investigation was to get to a strong motivating consumer truth in order to shape the advertising brief, while making the briefing process more engaging and

FIGURE 4.1   Previous approach to TV communication message (Indonesia)

rooted in real consumer behaviour. In emerging markets, the communications objective was to persuade non-treating sensitivity sufferers to treat, whereas in developed markets (Australia, USA and UK), the objective tended to be more about driving loyalty or usage frequency.

Success through good practice

The programme has been highly effective because of the behaviours it encouraged, as well as reflecting strong insight management and research practice. The global Sensodyne insight team have demonstrated leadership not only through crafting a programme that could be localized, but also through strong partnership with both local Sensodyne brand teams and Grey, the advertising agency. Along the way, Grey, Spinach and Sensodyne's global brand team co-created stimulus material that helped uncover better consumer truths and find the appropriate persuasion voice for the brand in each culture. Figure 4.2 shows the revised relevancy approach to TV communications in the Indonesian market.

FIGURE 4.2 The new relevancy driving approach (Indonesia)

Impact of the relevancy campaign

The relevancy campaign had a hugely positive impact on brand performance.

Indonesian market performance

The relevancy campaign has been running in Indonesia since April 2014, giving Sensodyne a rebound in performance. Consumption in Indonesia increased by 17 per cent (July 2014 vs July 2013), driving growth across the core range. Market share reached a record high of 6.7 per cent.

Thailand market performance

Since the relevancy campaign's launch in Thailand in May 2014, consumption has increased, on average by 20 per cent (vs three months previous). Sensodyne achieved its highest ever market share of 8.2 per cent in July 2014. There have been significant increases in penetration, reaching 7 per cent (July 2014 YTD) vs 4.5 per cent (Apr 2014 YTD).

Philippines market performance

The brand sustained a market share high for the year in which the new relevancy communications launched at 2.5 per cent (May–August 2014 vs 2.3 per cent in January–April 2014), moving its position from No 6 toothpaste brand at the start of the year to No 4 toothpaste brand since April 2014, overtaking Pepsodent and Unique.

Some of the key factors in the programme's success are outlined below.

The programme was built on effective insight management

During the early market investigations, it became clear that there were commonalities emerging in relation to how people experience tooth sensitivity pain and the intrusion it can have on their daily lives. Rather than begin each subsequent market exploration with a sense of the unknown, we started to gather and review what was consistently true of markets that had gone before, so that we could build on this further by generating hypotheses about what might be relevant and worthy of investigation in each new market. Following the first three market investigations (Philippines, Indonesia and India), it was possible to create a framework for life impact themes that we were confident held some universal truth. However, the pinpointing and expression of these themes would require local sensitivity to arrive at and it was important we remained open to new dimensions appearing as well.

Good insight management is at the heart of the programme because each new market undertaken has the benefit of building on the insights and knowledge generated in the previous markets. Much of the insight gathered in the earlier markets (Philippines, Indonesia, China, India and Australia) has been consolidated and now exists within the programme's body of reference material. This has helped make up a physical and virtual toolkit that also contains:

- the research plan;
- timing guidance;
- templates;
- tips on workshopping, research;
- key moments for collaboration between global and local brand teams and their partner, Grey;
- roles and responsibilities at key stages.

Insight ownership by highly experienced stakeholders

A strong sense of insight ownership at a high level of both GSK Consumer Healthcare and Grey was also instrumental to the success of the programme. Sensodyne's Global Marketing Director, Global Insight Team and Grey's SVP were all highly engaged during the initial markets, each functioning as insight contributors and keepers. This engagement enabled efficient decision making and pragmatism about when there was enough evidence to make a decision versus pausing to conduct primary research. In the initial markets investigated (Philippines and Indonesia), Spinach played a continuity role as an insight partner before progressing to help the Global Insight team develop the legacy programme itself.

The challenge

Encouraging participants to treat their tooth sensitivity (at all, or more frequently) requires more than brand expertise and advanced product technology. An understanding of what prevents sufferers from treating (as well as what triggers treaters to act), and how treatment could really impact on their lives, is crucial to persuasion. Sensitivity itself is a source of tension in people's lives but the fleeting nature and lure of other oral care benefits can result in de-prioritization of treatment. This leads to people putting up with intrusive pain or resorting to coping strategies – all of which can compromise their food and drink enjoyment. Understanding how to convince participants to tackle a problem they're already trying to deal with or are playing down is always a challenge; attempting to do this compellingly across cultures where eating habits, social mores, pain and health behaviours and attitudes vary widely makes the challenge even tougher.

Putting consumer insight at the heart of the advertising brief

While there are some similarities at the human truth level between markets around the experiences of tooth sensitivity, there is no 'one size fits all' approach to how best to put across a life impact benefit. As a result, the need to identify a tailored, market-specific consumer truth for each advertising brief was significant. Commonalities cannot even be assumed across a region – we found very different treatment barriers and sources of persuasion were required between Indonesia, India and China.

Insight gathering: Four key stages

Insight management drove the key stages of investigation in each market. The four key stages of insight gathering and channelling had their own objectives:

- Stage 1: Gather and review.
- Stage 2: Generate ideas.
- Stage 3: Explore the ideas.
- Stage 4: Write the advertising brief.

Stage 1 was principally about intelligence gathering. The Insight team would initially identify what they had available, logging all potential sources and disseminating key documents for review. Local market stakeholders and the global teams would each hold a download session to capture what they knew, generate hypotheses and establish where the knowledge gaps lay. If an

FIGURE 4.3   The ignite process overview

STAGE 1	STAGE 2	STAGE 3	STAGE 4
Gather Intelligence	Generate Ideas	Explore the Ideas	Write the Brief

STAGE 1 — Gather Intelligence

LOG OF POTENTIAL SOURCES

ALL GLOBAL & LOCAL STUDY OPTIONS LISTED

LOCAL SIMPLY TO TRACK DOWN & TICK ALL SOURCES ACCESSIBLE

WHAT DO WE HAVE?

REVIEW THE DATA

IDEALLY CIRCULATE KEY PIECES & HOLD A LOCAL DOWNLOAD SESSION

CAPTURE KEY TAKE-OUTS

WHAT DO WE KNOW?

ESTABLISH ANY GAPS

WHAT ELSE USEFUL TO KNOW

NEED TO PAUSE & COMMISSION RESEARCH?

WHAT DON'T WE KNOW?

STAGE 2 — Generate Ideas

CULTURAL SNAPSHOT– LOCAL

COMPLETE A SHORT PRESENTATION ON CULTURAL INSIGHTS, INCLUDING FOOD/DRINK HABITS, FAMILY, SOCIAL CLASS DYNAMICS

HYPOTHESES GLOBAL & LOCAL EACH HOLD 2HR WORKSHOP

GENERATE CONSUMER HYPOTHESES – IMMERSE IN DATA/FILMS & CULTURE

IDENTIFY POTENTIAL INSIGHT TERRITORIES

ADCEPT STIMULUS

LOCAL & GLOBAL HOLD A SESSION TOGETHER TO EITHER GENERATE INSIGHT STATEMENTS OR GENERATE ADCEPT IDEAS, WORKING WITH GLOBAL

BUILDING ON GLOBAL INSIGHT STATEMENT OR ADCEPT DECKS

STAGE 3 — Explore the Ideas

INTERNAL EXPLORATION

HOLD 1 DAY WORKSHOP TO EXPLORE/REFINE THE CONNECTION STIMULUS GENERATED

IDENTIFY MOST POWERFUL INSIGHT AREA

AND IF NEEDED, ALSO

EXTERNAL EXPLORATION OPTION

HEALTH HUB TO EXPLORE ADCEPTS

OR

QUAL TO EXPLORE INSIGHT STATEMENTS OR ADCEPTS

AND/OR

HOLD HALF-DAY SESSION ON DEBRIEF AND TO AGREE NEXT STEPS

IDENTIFY KEY COMMS INSIGHTS TO TAKE FORWARD

STAGE 4 — Write the Brief

GLOBAL & GREY TO FORMULATE THE BRIEF WITH LOCAL BUY-IN

in-depth understanding of consumer lures/barriers and language were missing, then primary qualitative research would typically be commissioned.

Stage 2 involved coming up with hypotheses and stimulus material that would uncover fertile communications territories or messages. The local market insight team would curate a short presentation on useful cultural insights and trends (including food/drink habits, family and social class dynamics) and circulate this within the global insight and Grey teams. The global and local brand teams, and advertising agency Grey, would then hold a video conference session or workshop to generate stimulus material that scoped out persuasion themes and tonality, the aim being to push the boundaries of consumer empathy and provocation and weave in a host of market-specific influences (relevant food/drinks, socializing dynamics, sense of humour, attitudes to enjoyment) so as to pinpoint the stronger persuasion elements at the consumer insight level.

Stage 3 focused on fine tuning or translating the stimulus before putting it into qualitative research – either face to face or using the GSK Consumer Healthcare online panel.

Stage 4 involved taking the results of the research done in stage 3 and agreeing the best strategy and expression, before briefing the ad agency accordingly.

Qualitative research driven by consumer-centric design

When there was a clear need for primary qualitative research (either because of knowledge gaps or because a response to some potential communications themes was needed), we went about the research with consumer empathy in mind. It can be the case, when leading up to advertising development, that stimulus is generated and put in front of participants (typically in qualitative research) in order to uncover what works best – and any previous stage of getting to really understand participants on their own terms can be leapfrogged. This can be a 'hit and miss' approach and may not get the best out of consumer engagement in the research process.

We used four key principles to ensure the research didn't impose ideas on participants, rather enabling them to shape their own input. These principles were:

1 Generate consumer language first.

2 Represent or adapt consumer language in the stimulus material.

3 Involve participants in the journey so they test their own ideas.

4 Enable participants to select what they're interested in.

Principle 1: Generate consumer language first

Tooth sensitivity has many different expressions and the condition itself isn't interpreted in the same way in different countries. It was important in the first phase of the programme, in markets where there were gaps in language understanding, to find out about beliefs, coping behaviours and experiences around tooth sensitivity. We used different methods to generate language so we didn't rely on one approach alone and we found we got different kinds of language contribution according to the research method. There were three techniques we tried out in parallel:

- peer interviewing in pairs;
- out of home face-to-face depth interviews;
- family member filming of consumption moments.

Peer interviewing in pairs

One of our hypotheses was that people might talk better with a close friend/ relative rather than with a researcher, so we paired up friends (one friend being a sensitivity sufferer who didn't treat with a sensitivity toothpaste, the other being their friend/neighbour or close relative who didn't suffer) and gave the non-sufferer a short guide to interview her friend with. The friendship dynamic and care conscience role that a concerned friend can adopt were really fruitful and elicited more colloquial language, emotions and human contradictions than we managed to generate from a more traditional moderator-led single depth interview. The friend was uniquely placed to challenge the sufferer about putting up with their sensitivity and interrogated them on why they perhaps hadn't ever mentioned it or adapted their behaviour, often missing out on treats. An experienced moderator would have had to have worked very hard to achieve this kind of rapport and may not have triggered some of the precious moments of personal realization. As a back-up, in case a pair lost their way or didn't stay on subject, we did have a moderator present but their role was much more backseat and guiding.

Out of home face-to-face depth interviews

We wanted some control over the language generation process so we also conducted some traditional F2F depth interviews. However, we hypothesized that we would learn more by placing sufferers in more of a 'torture test' situation, which was why we interviewed out of home in cafés. The foods and drinks that trigger sensitivity are often treats and we knew that the treat status and social exposure that goes with dining out would raise the stakes and highlight sensitivity sufferers' dilemmas, compromises and longing.

Family member filming of consumption moments

We were keen to capture some live moments of sensitivity pain striking, in order to see what triggered this and how people coped. We also wanted our sufferers to try and describe their experience 'in the moment' so the language was more accurate and heartfelt. Practically, we didn't feel this would work if we got participants to self-film because they would need their hands free to eat/drink and express themselves and we anticipated they might adapt their behaviour/expression if they felt especially self-conscious.

As a work-around, we enlisted the help of a family member (typically a teenage son/daughter) to assume the role of a documentary film-maker – filming eating/drinking moments over a period of time and asking their parent how they felt to draw out language. This proved highly effective because we witnessed body and facial language as well as verbal expression – also because this was conducted in-home in the presence of a close family member, the sufferer was less guarded and behaved more freely.

Principle 2: Represent or adapt consumer language in the stimulus material

Authenticity lies at the heart of the Sensodyne brand – and is essential to the success of the expert-led communications which feature unscripted, real testimony of dentists or scientists. Similarly, we didn't want to put words into participants' mouths during the research process so we generated statements or 'adcepts' (stimulus resembling concise print advertising examples composed of a headline, image and subtext) that featured verbatim comments and direct consumer language. We found the stimulus tended to be highly effective at generating conversation in group discussions and it helped us to identify key barriers to treatment as well as more persuasive angles to drive treatment.

Principle 3: Involve participants in the journey so they test their own ideas

When we had initiated a language-gathering phase of qualitative research, we reconvened these participants into group discussions and shared with them the stimulus material that they had essentially helped to generate. In this way, we played back to participants what we had heard from them in order to identify what best represents their feelings, language and behaviours. The other benefit to this approach was the priming effect of the first phase – this meant that the participants' self awareness was heightened during the subsequent groups, allowing them to tune into real experiences and not rely on recall or speculation.

Principle 4: Enable participants to select what they're interested in

The group discussions were run in a gallery style, and structured so as to enable participants to have time to digest and select the stimulus that best spoke to them on a personal level. The conversation areas were then prioritized according to themes that the participants selected. This meant that participants were discussing material they related to as individuals rather than being put in a more responsive position of having to react to stimulus we imposed upon them as a group. It also had the benefit of enabling coverage of a wider range of themes and expressions in order to better pinpoint what worked, or filter out what didn't work.

Conclusion

Sensodyne have seen the impact of culturally adapting their communications with local consumer insights at the centre of each new advertising brief. All markets undergoing the programme have since produced more effective communications and a sales uplift. This could not have been achieved without sophisticated insight management by Alexandra Wren and Mita Shaha in the GSK Consumer Healthcare Global Insight team, the senior stakeholder commitment to engage with the insight development right at the start and the vision to invest in a process that could become efficient and be delegated – while still delivering sharp consumer insight. Along the way, there have also been great examples of sound qualitative research practice and the growth of an insight community across the Sensodyne team worldwide, Grey and Spinach.

We can get to those hard to reach places

The world's most experienced b2b research specialist. By far.

At B2B International, we've carried out more b2b research studies, in more languages, in more markets, than anyone. So, we have an unrivalled understanding of the questions to ask, the people to talk to, and the decisions that need to be taken.
Find out how we can make our experience count for you.

www.b2binternational.com

Beyond Knowledge

Manchester / London / Düsseldorf / New York / Chicago / Shanghai / Beijing / Singapore

Understanding and accounting for cultural bias in global b2b research

05

While cultural bias is almost impossible to completely eliminate, as researchers we must take account of it when working with data, explains Conor Wilcock of B2B International.

The positive experience index

In late 2012, Gallup reported the findings of the Positive Experience Index, part of its World Poll, an annual survey of almost 150,000 people in 148 countries. According to the article, the poll found Singaporeans to be the least emotional and least positive of all nationalities (Clifton, 2012). Other countries appearing in the bottom 10 in terms of positive emotions reported included Iraq, Syria, Afghanistan and Haiti. But the data was clear: Singapore trumped them all, and was home to the least positive emotions and experiences in the world. On the other side of the coin, citizens of Latin America were positively squirming with joy and emotion: the top three 'happiest' countries according to Gallup were Panama, Paraguay and El Salvador (which incidentally has one of the world's highest homicide rates) (Overseas Security Advisory Council, 2014).

Singapore

Singapore is a country with the fourth highest Gross Domestic Product (GDP) per capita in the world, in terms of the Purchasing Power Parity (PPP) (World Bank, 2013). It's a country with virtually full employment (Singapore Ministry, 2014). It is home to a 'Hug Me' Coca Cola vending machine, which will kindly dispense a soda can once it receives a heartfelt embrace from the thirsty consumer (*Huffington Post*, 2012).

The chances are that getting a hug and a Coke at the same time renders few people emotionless and melancholy. Some from academic and intellectual circles expressed a little scepticism, and the utility of the positive index survey was critiqued by researchers, psychologists and, most probably, by Singaporeans themselves (Lallanilla, 2012). They argued that the results of the poll tell us less about how happy people are and more about cultural traits when it comes to displaying emotions and responding to surveys. Is it really that Singaporeans are less happy than everyone else? Or is it rather that they are less likely to communicate positive emotions? Or that they provide fewer strong/extreme responses to polls and surveys than Latin Americans? Gallup itself makes the important and related point that Latin Americans have a 'cultural tendency...to focus on the positives in life'. (Clifton, 2014).

Cultural survey bias

This light-hearted case study draws attention to the subject of cultural survey bias: participants of different nationalities respond in a variety of ways to surveys, in part due to cultural factors. This topic has been discussed at length in consumer research circles, and in the academic sphere of social psychology, but the conversation has, as of yet, remained very much on the fringes of b2b research. The purpose of this paper is to focus the debate of cultural survey bias in a business-to-business research context.

Why is it important to approach cultural survey bias from a b2b perspective? B2b organizations are increasingly challenged with reaching a global and diverse target audience. In order for insights to be actionable across borders, researchers and marketers should be aware of the cultural biases that are at play when conducting research in business-to-business markets. An 'apples to apples' comparison of multi-country survey data can lead to skewed findings and actions built on bias, not knowledge.

Put simply: those apples you're comparing against each other? They're not all the same.

An introduction to survey response styles

Charles Kettering, once head of research for GM, said that 'a problem well stated is a problem half-solved'. Simply being aware of and understanding the cultural biases which exist in market research is as important as identifying ways of accounting and reducing such biases. Research conducted by B2B International on cultural bias using numerical rating scales has found that a participant's culture primarily affects the relative strength of three response styles:

- **Extreme Response:** This is the tendency for a participant to select the extreme ratings on a scale. For a 1–10 scale, this generally means 1–4 and 9–10.

- **Midpoint Response:** This is the tendency for a participant to select the middle ratings on a scale. For a 1–10 scale, this generally means 5–8.

- **Acquiescence:** This is the inclination to agree with the interviewer/ survey sponsor, or to respond in such a way that will 'please' them.

Participant groups with a strong Extreme Response usually produce higher mean scores and indexes, eg overall satisfaction and Net Promoter Score (NPS).[1] This is because positive feedback in surveys usually outweighs negative feedback. Therefore, countries which tend towards the Extreme Response are often seen at the high end of country-ranked results. On the other hand, the Midpoint Response style usually leads to lower mean scores and indexes, at the low end of country-ranked results.

High acquiescence usually results in higher scores, as the participant's belief is that a higher rating is a positive result for the survey sponsor. There is less evidence of strong acquiescence bias in b2b research than in consumer research, as participant seniority comes into effect. So the more senior the participant is, the lower the acquiescence bias. Owing to cultural factors, however, acquiescence bias among participants with the same seniority will differ by country, eg a CFO in France versus a CFO in Brazil.

Cultural bias: the results

Plotted in Figure 5.1 is a summary of cultural bias in b2b research, in terms of different response styles.

Latin America

In Latin American markets (primarily Brazil and Mexico), participants are likely to adopt an Extreme Response style, with high acquiescence towards the survey sponsor or interviewer. In most global satisfaction, loyalty and branding studies, these are the countries which score highest. This very much mirrors the cultural biases at play in consumer research (nine of the top ten 'happiest' countries according to Gallup's poll were in Central or South America).

FIGURE 5.1   Cultural bias in b2b research

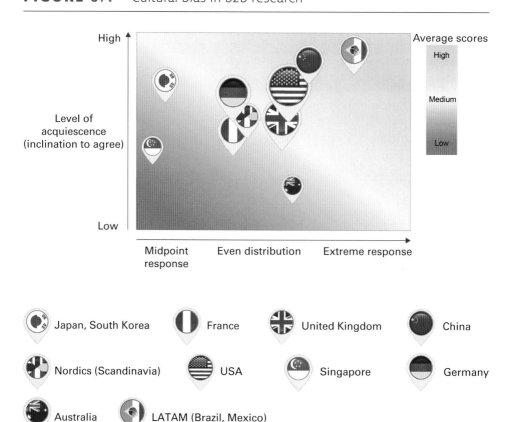

China

Chinese participants also tend towards high acquiescence bias, but have a slightly more even distribution of scores on the rating scale, ie using all parts of the scale. Over the last five years, Chinese survey response has shifted slightly away from the Extreme Response style, potentially as a result of increased collaboration with Western businesses, and also because b2b participants are becoming more attuned to market research.

USA

Being the first and primary b2b research market, it is unsurprising that participants in the US have a fairly even distribution response style. US participants elicit a higher acquiescence bias than Western Europeans, but results in the US are the closest of any country to the satisfaction and loyalty benchmarks that researchers have long considered to be 'global'.

Western Europe

Like the US, most Western European markets have an even response distribution that utilizes all parts of the rating scale. However, we see lower acquiescence bias in the UK and France, which leads to slightly lower scores overall.

Australia

Australian participants provide some of the lower aggregate scores of any country, but these are due primarily to very low acquiescence bias, rather than an Extreme or Midpoint Response. This also means that the client 'bump' evident in other countries (where the survey sponsor receives higher scores than competitors) is much less of a factor in Australia.

South East Asia

Interestingly, participants in Japan and Korea adopt very different response styles from those in China. Although still exhibiting a mid-to-high acquiescence bias, participants in these countries focus heavily on the midpoint ratings (5–8), which, when aggregated, lead to lower average scores than in other countries.

Singapore

Circling back to the Singaporeans, our b2b dataset certainly follows a similar pattern to the Gallup World Poll result. These participants have the strongest tendency to the Midpoint Response style of all markets tested. Singapore also exhibited mid-to-low acquiescence bias, resulting in low aggregate scores.

Trends and contributing factors

Researchers, of course, should avoid making 'broad brush' conclusions about cultural bias, without first taking into account other factors which may affect response styles within and among cultures. We also must appreciate that the research world is constantly changing, as are the ways in which participants approach surveys and rating scales. An understanding of these trends is critical in any attempt to account for and address cultural bias in global studies.

Survey language

Generally, native language interviews produce a stronger Extreme Response Style, while non-native language interviewing (eg English in Scandinavia) produces a stronger Midpoint Response Style. For example, a survey conducted with Norwegian participants in English is more likely to lead to lower aggregate scores than if the surveys were administered in Norwegian.

Survey methodology

We see higher levels of acquiescence bias with more 'direct' survey methodologies, ie those which involve the presence of an interviewer, who administers the questions. Telephone interviews result in higher acquiescence bias than online surveys, with acquiescence in face-to-face interviews higher still.

The effect that the survey methodology has on acquiescence bias is more pronounced in countries with high online penetration. In Latin America, online research produces high acquiescence bias anyway, whereas in the United States all-but-universal online penetration means that levels of acquiescence are more greatly increased when direct methodologies are used.

Cultural bias influenced by survey method is important to consider, especially in b2b projects for which a mixed methodology is employed. So we might expect to see higher aggregate scores for the telephone sample, than for those surveyed online.

Differences between b2b and b2c response styles

A comparison of cultural bias studies conducted in consumer circles with our analysis of b2b research shows similar results. This makes sense, considering that every business decision maker is a consumer when they leave for work in the morning and return home in the evening. Cultural biases should – and do – circumvent the work/home threshold. However, there are key differences when examining response styles of b2b versus consumer participants within countries.

Generally speaking, b2b participants are less likely to provide extremely positive or negative ratings on a survey scale. This could be due to the longer-term relationships which exist in b2b markets; such tenured interactions could lead to a smoothening out of scaled responses, because of the expected ups and downs of such a relationship.

Our theory is supported by looking at the range of Net Promoter Scores for consumer brands versus b2b brands. Generally, the worst-performing consumer brands receive lower Net Promoter Scores than their b2b equivalents (imagine the energy company or internet service provider which makes your blood boil). The story is the same with the best-performing brands. When conducting business-to-business-to-consumer (b2b2c) studies which include consumer and business participants within one country, researchers may anticipate more bunched responses among the b2b sample.

The effect of 'westernization' on response styles in developing markets

Our analysis uncovered some interesting shifts over time. B2b survey response styles across many parts of the world are changing, and research and analysis from B2B International has uncovered that this is happening most notably in developing markets, potentially as a result of businesses in these regions having more interaction with western firms. Nowhere was this shift more notable than in China. Response styles among Chinese b2b participants have become less extreme over the last three to five years, and now more closely mirror the likes of the US and UK. We might expect to see a similar shift for Mexico and Brazil, as they do more business with Western countries and as b2b research becomes more entrenched and less of a 'novelty'.

A significant and related challenge in measuring the impact of cultural bias on survey response styles has been brought about by b2b migration, ie individuals from one country relocating to work in other countries. Such cultural workplace integration can 'muddy the waters' pertaining to measuring cultural bias in b2b research, and is most evident in such regions as North America, South East Asia and the Middle East, where the proportion of migrant workers is higher than elsewhere in the world (ILO, 2015).

Accounting for participant seniority

Generally speaking, the more senior the participant, the more they will exhibit a midpoint response style and the less they will exhibit acquiescence bias. This typically leads to lower aggregate scores when compared with those in junior roles in the same country.

This distinction is more apparent in countries which typically have stricter and more linear business hierarchies. In China for example businesses often operate a Confucian hierarchy, where senior executives are 'benevolent leaders'. The fall in acquiescence bias, when surveying a senior participant, is therefore, greater in China than it is in Scandinavia or Australia, where the hierarchies are more casual (or even non-existent). Interestingly, in these countries we see a lower inclination to agree with, or please, the interviewer or survey sponsor in general.

Attempts to reduce or eliminate cultural bias

So what can be done about this? Is it possible to reduce cultural bias, or at least reduce the impact it has on conclusions for global research programs? Or do we have to accept the role it plays in b2b research, learning to *live with it*, like a slightly annoying room-mate?

There are some different ways in which researchers may attempt to reduce the impact of cultural bias on data.

Scale anchoring

Researchers can reduce confusion and to a certain extent cultural bias by anchoring numerical scales, to ensure clear and objective definitions are communicated to participants of all nationalities. In a satisfaction survey, this generally means '1 – not at all satisfied' and '10 – completely (or extremely) satisfied'. Without anchoring, researchers put themselves at the whim of participant subjectivity: a score of 7 out of 10 will be interpreted very differently in Japan than it is in Brazil.

Anchoring also avoids participant confusion as to which end of the scale is positive and which is negative. In German schools, for example, outstanding students are given a score of 1. Therefore, many Germans enter adulthood with the subconscious perception that 1 equals the best score possible. We certainly would not recommend flipping a rating scale for German participants only in a multi-country survey; however, clear anchoring should serve to eliminate inaccurate grading.

The importance of 'going native'

Generally, native language interviews result in more extreme responses, while non-native language interviewing (eg English in the Netherlands) results in more midpoint responses. For example, a survey conducted with Dutch participants in English is more likely to lead to lower aggregate scores than if the surveys were administered in Dutch. This might be because people feel more confident responding in their native tongue and are therefore more likely to answer assertively.

Rather than adopting English as the default language for global surveys, researchers should seek to administer them in native languages. Although this will not eliminate cultural bias, it will lessen the negative skew in the data caused by strong midpoint responses.

The dangers of 'standardizing' results

It may be tempting for researchers to attempt to eliminate cultural bias from research datasets by applying weighted algorithms, with the intention of standardizing the results. For example, researchers could utilize an algorithm based on typical response styles which may shift a company's Net Promoter Score up or down according to each different country in which it operates.

However, arbitrary formulations of this nature can be damaging to research and subsequent action plans, as they are determinist and reductionist. Increasing Japan's Net Promoter Score by 35 points and reducing Mexico's by 20 – to use a basic example – throws aside the possibility that other factors (biases as well as the company's actual performance) may be at play. It's incredibly difficult to quantify the effect of one bias, and impossible to quantify the cumulative effects of all biases in a survey. Therefore, ensuring sampling consistency is the only way to account for and to control cultural bias over time.

Conclusion: 'A problem well-stated'

The key point here is that cultural bias is almost impossible to completely eliminate, and that's not a terrible thing. Bias that we acknowledge can be accounted for and, though it may remain in some form, it is a bias we can control (or at least we can control the impact it has on our research findings). Unacknowledged bias is beyond our control and can damage the validity of market research. Martha Heineman Pieper's work on research in the social work field argues that 'it is better to recognize and manage [biases]... than to deny or overlook them' (Heineman Pieper, 2002).

As researchers, our primary goal is to ensure that data is as actionable as possible, while maintaining high levels of reliability and validity. If we accept cultural bias as an unfortunate but inevitable part of multi-country research, the most appropriate action we can take is to account for it when analysing and interpreting data. Three primary ways to do so are as follows:

1. Global versus local

Researchers should avoid using 'global' benchmarks to drive 'local' action. Take the Net Promoter Score, for example. Benchmarks for the Net Promoter Score have generally favoured Western audiences, eg using data from participants in the US, UK and Germany. Although these markets are the largest for b2b research, researchers should be careful not to apply such benchmarks to studies which go beyond these countries. If a Client's Net Promoter Score in Japan is below the 'global' benchmark, it is not necessarily indicative of a pandemic. It could be that customer loyalty in Japan has improved from the previous year, but applying the 'global' to inform the 'local' will muddy the waters.

2. In-country trending

Utilizing trending data within a particular country enables researchers to draw reliable conclusions from tracking studies, eg Japan Wave 1 versus Japan Wave 2, rather than Japan Wave 2 versus USA Wave 2.

Even when isolating the results from one country, researchers should be aware of in-country cultural biases, such as ethnicity (eg Hispanic versus Caucasian response tendencies), religion, participant seniority, gender, and other demographics and firmographics. These biases are beyond the scope of this paper, but they are very much at play in research studies.

3. Sampling consistency

What in-country trending and local benchmarking cannot solve is the issue of global aggregate tracking, a critical metric for many business-to-business research users. If a company's global Net Promoter Score shifts downward one year, how can we be certain that the shift is to do with a decline in performance and not a sampling difference, eg higher numbers of Korean or Australian participants, or fewer Chinese? By establishing quotas for tracking studies, researchers can ensure that the impact of cultural bias in historical trending data is accounted for and that wave-to-wave results shifts are not due to sampling changes. For example, it is important to ensure that, in each wave, the sample is evenly divided by country/region.

As business-to-business research becomes more global, understanding cultural bias and applying that understanding to research findings, is critical in ensuring that actions taken are based on real insight. The next time you ask a b2b participant how satisfied they are with a product or service, think about the cultural factors that might be influencing the way they answer. Their '8 out of 10' might not mean the same as the next person's.

How do you like them apples?

References

Clifton, J (2012) *Latin Americans Most Positive in the World*, December 19. Retrieved from www.gallup.com/poll/159254/latin-americans-positive-world.aspx2e2e2e

Clifton, J (2014) *People Worldwide Are Reporting a Lot of Positive Emotions.* May 2. Retrieved from www.gallup.com/poll/169322/people-worldwide-reporting-lot-positive-emotions.aspx

Heineman Pieper, M, Heineman Pieper, J and Tyson McCrea, K (2002) Doing good science without sacrificing good values: Why the heuristic paradigm is the best choice for social work, *Families In Society, 83* (1), pp 15–28. Retrieved from http://ecommons.luc.edu/cgi/viewcontent.cgi?article=1010&context=socialwork_facpubs

Huffington Post (2012) Coke machine takes hugs instead of money. April 11. Retrieved from www.huffingtonpost.com/2012/04/11/hug-coke-machine_n_1418383.html

International Labor Organization (2015). *ILO Global Estimates On Migrant Workers*. Retrieved from www.ilo.org/wcmsp5/groups/public/--dgreports/--dcomm/documents/publication/wcms_436343.pdf

Lallanilla, M (2012) *Happiest Nations on Earth Revealed*, December 20. Retrieved from www.livescience.com/25713-happiest-countries-happiness-gallup.html

Overseas Security Advisory Council (2014, June 3). *El Salvador 2014 Crime and Safety Report*. Retrieved from www.osac.gov/pages/ContentReportDetails.aspx?cid=15771

Singapore Ministry of Manpower (2014) *Employment Situation*, Second Quarter, 31 July 31. Retrieved from www.mom.gov.sg/newsroom/Pages/PressReleasesDetail.aspx?listid=581

The World Bank (2013) *GDP per capita, PPP (current international $)*. Retrieved from http://data.worldbank.org/indicator/NY.GDP.PCAP.PP.CD?order=wbapi_data_value_2013+wbapi_data_value+wbapi_data_value-last&sort=desc

Reference

1 The Net Promoter Score (NPS) is a metric widely used in market research, which measures levels of advocacy of a specific company. Participants are asked to rate their likelihood of recommending the company on a scale (typically 0 to 10, but 1 to 10 scales are also used). The Net Promoter Score is calculated by subtracting the proportion of brand 'detractors' (those rating 6 or below) from the proportion of brand 'promoters' (those rating 9 or 10). The result is a score ranging from −100 to +100.

The challenges of media research

06

Behavioural economics teaches us the importance of the context within which people act, and this is vital for effective market research and communication, as Simon Shaw of Trinity McQueen explains.

The growth of media channels

Media owners use research to prove that their media channels work and are good value to their customers, the advertisers. Advertisers rely on research to show that advertising has worked both creatively and in terms of media choice. Both need to understand how people use media and receive messages. This sets the challenge for media research. It must overcome two issues in order to be useful.

First, there are many media channels and people are exposed to many of them either simultaneously (surfing social media on their phone while watching TV) or over time (the newspaper in the morning, the radio in the car, the letter on the doormat when they come home). Research needs to attribute effects correctly to each channel and observe when combined effects are stronger.

Second, people are prone to misattributing the role of advertising in their lives. Primarily they forget or dismiss most of what they are exposed to. What they do recall and remember they often wrongly attribute to what they assume are more dominant media channels. TV often gets the credit that press, posters, online and direct mail in part deserve.[1]

The growth of both 'traditional' media (more TV channels, DAB radio, free papers) and 'new' media (news brands online, social media, online advertising, etc) has created ever greater fragmentation. This only makes the task of market research harder. While some new media have metrics 'baked in' such as the measure of clicks, views, likes, tweets etc, this can create a misattribution of its own where the easy to measure, but less effective, is favoured over the hard-to-measure but more effective.[2]

New techniques for media research

Media research will always rely in part on people's recall of advertising. This remains a quick and cheap way of roughly measuring success. However, in recent years, approaches based on academic advances in neuroscience and behavioural economics have both helped move beyond this reliance on recall, and can help solve the problems of misattribution.

Techniques adopted from neuroscience and biometrics mean we can now say with confidence which messages are likely to form lasting memories and go on to influence future behaviour. Behavioural economics has inspired experiments that isolate the underlying influences on behaviour, providing clear evidence of what participants are unable to attribute or struggle to recall. This methodological precision is made possible by advances in recording technologies which make ethnography, self-ethnography and observation cheaper and less intrusive.

Case studies

The two case studies outlined in this chapter both use innovations in methodology driven by neuroscience and behavioural economics to solve the problem of advertising misattribution – a core issue for advertising mail. The cases describe how Trinity McQueen worked with Royal Mail MarketReach (the part of Royal Mail that supports advertisers' use of mail) to understand how mail, leaflets and catalogues work as advertising media.

The first case study shows how we used CCTV and ethnography to evidence what actually happens to mail in the home: where it goes, how long it lives and what it is used for. We have highlighted several learnings for qualitative research design, particularly when leveraging technology.

The second case study shows how we combined a controlled experiment and neuroscience to evidence the impact of the *medium* on the message. The quality of paper shouldn't affect the desire to read something, but it does. We have highlighted several learnings for behavioural research design.

CASE STUDY 1 The private life of mail

Ask people what they do with advertising mail and most say they ignore it. The narrative of 'junk mail' dominates direct questioning. Yet, when behaviour is examined, every £1 spent on advertising mail delivers on average a £3.22 return on investment.[3] We've all witnessed people opening, saving and responding to advertising mail. People just don't talk about this in market research. Mail sorting and opening is often habitual, something people do on autopilot – without the attention that produces recall and attribution.

This is a real image problem for the medium. Advertising mail contracts are an important part of Royal Mail's business: this problem of misattribution is not merely a research issue, but one that means their business is losing out to other media channels based on mis-understandings and myths.

Trinity McQueen and Royal Mail set out to prove the impact of mail. This meant capturing people's private, unguarded moments – the points where they were acting without thinking. Our goal was to educate advertisers about the unique properties of mail in our increasingly digital world. We did so by observing people living their lives:

- how people really interact with advertising mail in their homes;

- understanding mail's unique properties in comparison to other media;

- how mail integrates with people's on- and off-line media lives.

Our approach

Our approach was based on the knowledge that people are poor witnesses to their own behaviour. Observation was crucial to bridge this attitude–behaviour gap. We were mindful however of the observer effect:[4] how our presence might change participants' behaviour. If participants knew we were interested in mail, for example, they might pay more attention to it, skewing results. We needed to ensure our observation methods were discrete and wouldn't distort mail behaviour.

Table 6.1 outlines the different approaches our research took to the three objectives of our research.

TABLE 6.1   The three objectives of our research outlines: different approaches

Research problem	Approach
Deliver an intimate understanding of how UK households use media	• A two-week ethnography of 12 UK households • All media use was explored. Mail was only revealed as the subject at the final visit
Measure what people do with mail, not just what they say	• CCTV cameras installed in main living areas of household for 3–7 days • Media use for each household member coded by day

Provide a nationally representative measure of mail behaviour	• Behavioural survey of 1129 UK participants
	• Media preferences established before subject of survey revealed
	• The survey asked participants about *specific, recent behaviour:*
	  – what they had done with that day's mail;
	  – asked to check the places in their household where they had saved previous mail to remind themselves of what was there, who it was from and how long it had been kept.
	• CCTV clips demonstrating different ways people interact with mail were shown. Participants self-identified which of these strategies they used in their lives

The ethics of observation in commercial ethnography

Having a stranger spend time in your home and leave cameras running to record your behaviour is an unusual request. For the project to be a success, we had to put participants first. This was not only about ensuring their informed consent but taking the time to put them at ease.

The head of each household was carefully screened; the lead researcher then talked them through the project. We couldn't reveal the project sponsor, but explained that the project was about mapping their household's media use in as much detail as possible. Participants were then sent a professionally designed information pack outlining what exactly what their involvement would require, and used this to seek the permission of their family in writing. Our first visit to participant homes was spent gaining their trust and reiterating the purpose of the study. Participants soon relaxed once we had shown them how the CCTV kit worked and got their assistance in placing the cameras in the living areas. Inevitably, we began as observers then as time went on rapport developed and we became observer-participants,[5] making tea and helping to feed children.

If you read any academic commentary on ethnography, it soon becomes apparent that there is at best suspicion, and at worst hostility, to commercial market researchers claiming to use ethnographic methods.[6] Although no comparison can be made to being embedded within a community for a year, as is the norm in academia,[7] any market researcher used to conducting both qualitative and ethnographic methods will know the nuanced understanding that spending extended periods of time with participants brings. Spending a day with a participant – about five times the length of a focus group – gives much more than five times as much depth. The benchmark therefore is not academic ethnography but 'in and out' techniques typical of market research, which used in isolation provide limited context or immersion.

FIGURE 6.1 The three objectives of our research outlines

Research findings

1. Mail use is instinctive: The average UK adult has negative attitudes towards advertising mail but actually displays positive behaviour. At Stage 1, 10 of our 12 participants said their household *'tends to ignore advertising mail sent in the post'*. However, CCTV revealed that *all* participants interacted with advertising mail in the observation period – this involved opening, reading, saving and responding to direct mail, catalogues and/or door drops. We captured priceless footage of real people engaged by advertising mail. It could be a spa brochure, home improvement flyer or detergent coupon, but upon questioning participants said they kept items because they were relevant and useful. Had the study relied on stated attitudes alone, the findings would have been very different.

FIGURE 6.2   CCTV footage of participants interacting with mail despite claiming to ignore it

"Free 8 wash trial pack? We'll have that!"

"What do you tend to do with advertising mail?"
"Recycling, it just goes straight outside..."

Our quantitative study replicated these findings. Stated attitudes show that around two-thirds of the UK population (65 per cent) '*tend to ignore advertising mail sent in the post*' yet of those who received a promotional letter or special offer in the post that day, two-thirds opened it (69 per cent).

People are not being consciously untruthful. Advertising mail may not even be perceived as advertising mail: targeted mail might be described as '*a letter from a company I've bought from before*' for example. Perception of behaviour is a common problem for researchers. When people say they don't do the thing you're asking about, they often do, just under another name; or they might not count it because it is the exception rather than the rule.

2. Mail is alive: The benefit of investing time with our households was a nuanced understanding of their media usage, something one or two visits would not have made possible. We could see that mail had a life within the home. Items we noticed on our first visit would often move to different locations on future visits (for example from mantelpiece to fridge door).

Most households have a 'gatekeeper' who gets to the mail first. What is not deemed relevant for the recipient is often saved for another member of the household. Mail is often sorted and then collected in a routine holding zone, for example, the living room table. Commonly, mail is then 'piled' in various locations familiar to household members. To attract the greatest attention, single items of mail are displayed as a reminder/incentive to act – for example on a computer keyboard. Some mail is then saved for a longer period, eg on fridges, mantelpieces, and windowsills. Our survey showed that people usually save mail in the kitchen (51 per cent) – most commonly attached to the fridge door by a magnet. It is arguable, therefore, that mail has a brand building effect, strengthening memory associations or what Byron Sharp calls 'mental availability'.[8] Mail becomes a media space in its own right around the home, like a series of mini-billboards. You can't do that with a Tweet.

FIGURE 6.3   Mail display

3. Mail works: CCTV evidence showed that people spend more time with mail than they realize. The momentary interactions that participants described in recollection often lasted between two and five minutes from doormat to living room when we examined CCTV evidence. Mail played a significant part in some participants' media consumption – something we did not predict at the outset of the project.

FIGURE 6.4   Weekday mail interactions for Katie

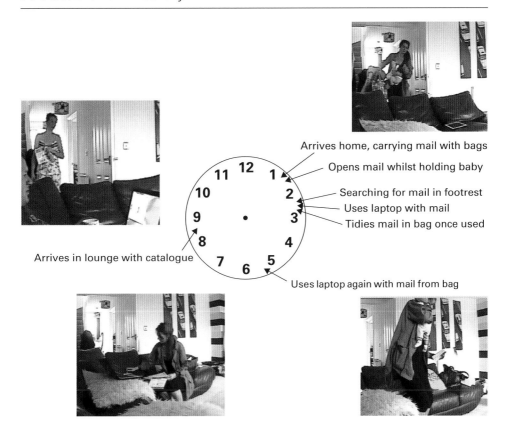

FIGURE 6.5   Average time interacting with mail by household

	Prefamily	Young family	Older family	Empty nester
Household 1	1 minute 55 seconds	6 minutes 30 seconds	32 minutes 22 seconds	12 minutes 46 seconds
Household 2	34 seconds	2 minutes 7 seconds	1 minute 3 seconds	7 minutes 25 seconds
Household 3	2 minutes 3 seconds	5 minutes 17 seconds	6 minutes 17 seconds	5 minutes 38 seconds

Asking participants to check the age of saved mail showed it is far from an ephemeral medium. Counter to the 'junk mail' narrative, items like restaurant vouchers or supermarket coupons provide real benefits and they are welcomed into the home. Our survey showed that saved advertising mail lives in the average UK home for 17 days. This compares favourably even to something unique like a wedding invitation, which on average would be kept for 27 days.

The outcome

Our methods evidenced the disparity between attitudes and behaviour.

Revealed preferences rather than *stated preferences* showed the private life of mail is richer even than we had assumed. Mail items displayed prominently can act like billboards in the home, with a long-term brand building effect. Response rates or attitudinal surveys are therefore a limited KPIs for mail, underestimating its effect.

The findings were summarized in an insight-based rationale for the top 3000 advertisers in the UK to use mail, representing major cultural change within Royal Mail.

Summary learnings for commercial ethnography

1 Start projects with firm hypotheses. This gives the research an edge.

2 Develop an observation guide to reduce subjectivity in the field. An observation guide goes beyond a typical discussion guide, incorporating hypotheses and checklists for the instinctive, ephemeral behaviour of note. We have even used body-language checklists for example. Preparation helps observation.

3 Ensure the project team is diverse. The emotional impact each researcher experiences as they spend time with participants is a key part of the knowledge we create. Simply put, diversity means better data.

4 An analysis session midway through fieldwork will develop and extend your hypotheses. Typically, they lead to team re-briefings and updated observation guides.

5 At Trinity McQueen we like to use a hypothesis grid to assist analysis and accelerate conclusion making. Participants are columns, hypotheses are rows – allowing an overview of the evidence. They also make nice colour-coded debrief slides.

6 Consider observer effects: your presence can change the behaviour you are trying to measure. Technology may act as your surrogate, removing this observer effect.

7 Technology, however, adds to the organizational and analysis burden. The wrong solution will offer limited incremental insight. Two suggestions: pilot methods and have clients review the deliverables. Use an off-the-shelf solution.

8 Ethnography is time intensive. You gather huge amounts of data and develop a nuanced understanding of your topic. A purchase journey described as linear in an in-depth interview is likely to be more complex when observed, percolating gradually or pinballing wildly between research, verification, trial and purchase. Allow yourself the time to document the complexity you have observed.

9 Perception of behaviour is a common problem for researchers. When people say that they don't do they thing you're asking about, they often do, just under another name; or they might not 'count' it because it is the exception rather than the rule. It is a reminder to measure behaviour then cross-reference attitudes.

10 Participant rapport will elevate your project. You have spent time decoding their behaviour. It may be appropriate to prompt participants with their behaviour at the end of the project. You don't have to agree with their interpretation, but these discussions may falsify or extend hypotheses (eg '*I only stopped using Facebook on my phone as I'd run out of credit*').

CASE STUDY 2   The medium and the message

It's been 50 years since Marshall McLuhan coined the phrase 'The medium is the message'. What he wanted to convey was that 'the form of a medium embeds itself in the message, creating a symbiotic relationship by which the medium influences how the message is perceived'.[9]

People know this intuitively. This is why couples spend time and effort creating their wedding invitations. When a wedding invitation lands on your doormat, the creamy heavyweight card, embossed writing, and thick envelope communicate a great deal about the event before you have even read who sent it. The object *primes* our interpretation of the message.

When developing a campaign using advertising mail, the production of the physical object is the last step in the creative process (proposition, idea, message and content, design and layout, production of object and then the consumer). If you skimp on production you may be undermining the effectiveness of your message. Marketers who do so may go on to blame the channel itself rather than the production. We wanted to explore this, aiming to prove the value of touch (tangibility) – the one characteristic that makes mail unique.

Trinity McQueen and Royal Mail created a controlled experiment, examining the medium of advertising mail itself. Our questions were simple:

- Which physical effects (eg weight, die-cutting, embossing) make a mail piece more effective?

- What difference does it make if you invest in a mail piece?

- What rules should an advertiser follow to maximize response?

Answering these questions was complex.

We needed to **bypass direct questioning** to understand physical effects. Opening mail is a habitual process: we set up a controlled experiment with participants opening their mail as they would in real life – with our stimulus mixed in. To *isolate* the physical effects we needed bespoke stimulus. We couldn't use real brands as existing brand preferences might drive participants' reaction, not the mail item itself.

Our experiment was a controlled test:

- Five fake brands were produced.

- Copy describing a product/service was created for each (current account, weekend break, skiing holiday, jeans, washing detergent).

- Five progressively more tangible versions of a direct mail piece were created for each brand.

FIGURE 6.6   Examples of each brand

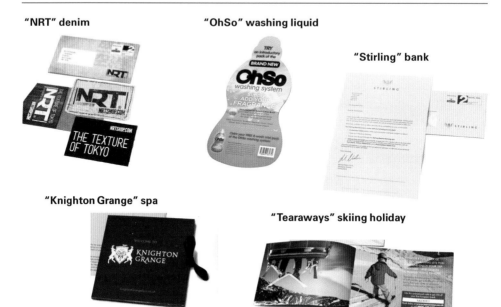

"NRT" denim

"OhSo" washing liquid

"Stirling" bank

"Knighton Grange" spa

"Tearaways" skiing holiday

FIGURE 6.7   Versions 1 and 5 of detergent brand 'OhSo'

Version 1	Version 5
	 Die-cut bottle shape Heavy card stock Foil embossed logo Scratch and sniff panel
Standard flyer on lightweight stock	

We tested this stimulus with a sample of 62 participants: a cross-section of the UK general public. This was a sizeable qualitative sample, allowing us to examine physical effects in detail: a precise sample design was created to ensure each participant saw one version of stimulus for each brand (eg bank version 1, washing liquid version 2 etc); a minimum of 12 participants saw each version of the stimulus (eg 12 saw bank v1, v2, v3, v4, v5 across the sample).

We triangulated three methodologies to get our data:

- **In-home observation**
  - warm-up interview
  - participants opening their own mail with our stimulus mixed in
  - real behaviour observed: dwell time and how items 'actioned' (eg discarded, voucher kept, saved for later)

- **Laboratory biometric and neuroscientific research**
  - eyetracking – to observe what participants look at, in what order
  - electroencephalography (EEG) and galvanic skin response (GSR) – to compare stated attitudes to emotional response. EEG measures electrical conductivity on the scalp. Participants wear a cap fitted with sensors that take readings from sites associated with cognitive functions such as emotional intensity, frustration and long-term memory encoding. GSR measures tiny fluctuations in your body temperature and perspiration. Based on the same technology as the fabled polygraph test of American cop dramas, participants wear a Wi-Fi enabled bracelet which takes readings from their wrist.

- **Self-completion questionnaires capturing reaction to mail pieces**
  - emotional impact
  - 'talkability' – spontaneous descriptions of each item.

Research findings

1 *Tangibility drives attention and emotional engagement – putting people in the right frame of mind to explore a mail piece.* The most tangible stimulus (eg those that used heavyweight paper, foiling, die-cutting, embossing etc) had longer dwell times, were more likely to be kept and responded to, and evoked stronger emotional responses.

FIGURE 6.8   OhSO detergent – the most tangible versions were most likely to be kept

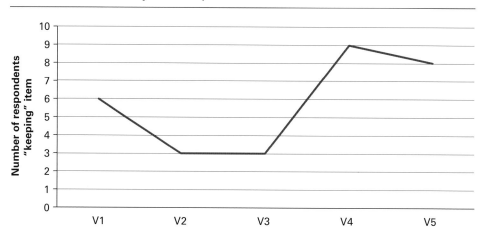

2 *Tangible mail pieces impose a lower cognitive load on people – easing decision making.* The EEG showed participants found it easier to interpret stimulus with physical effects. It was more obvious what was being advertised.

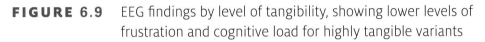

FIGURE 6.9   EEG findings by level of tangibility, showing lower levels of frustration and cognitive load for highly tangible variants

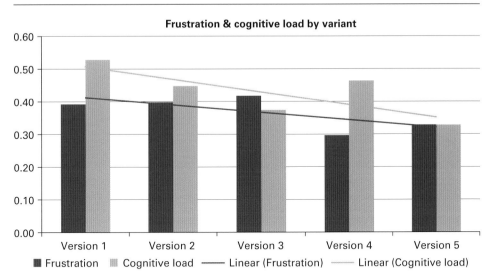

3   *The tangible properties of mail pieces are transmitted to the service being advertised – people subconsciously conflate the physical with the actual.* Handling tangible stimulus variants made participants:

- more able to describe the stimulus (they had more to say about it);

- more likely to express brand attributes eg luxury;

- more positive towards the brands. Semantic analysis showed participant descriptions were more positive, less functional and more emotive for highly tangible stimulus.

The conclusion: people conflate the physical (eg high quality card) with the actual brand advertised (eg posh). As one participant put it: 'This information *feels* expensive'.

FIGURE 6.10   Spontaneous descriptions – positive & emotional for the most tangible stimulus, neutral & functional for the least

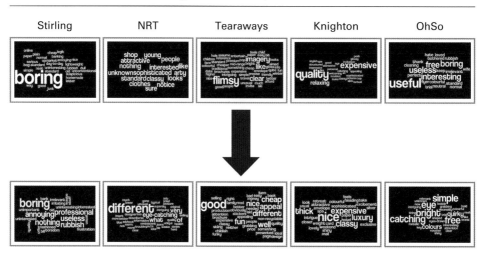

4   *Category disinterest trumps tangibility.* The most tangible mail pieces (Version 5s) performed better than the most basic counterparts (Version 1s), but the category was also important. For example, participants who did not ski were unlikely to engage with the skiing mail piece, regardless of tangibility. It follows, therefore, that producing beautiful mail can only increase inherent interest. This is a good thing: after all, you wouldn't want people who aren't interested in your services responding to your campaign.

Interpretation of findings

We are cognitive misers.[10] The counter intuitive truth is that in many cases *not* thinking about something is preferable to thinking about it. Rules of thumb work well most of the time and are quicker and easier than thinking.

When marketers craft communications they focus their efforts disproportionately on their message. They assume that their message is so important, clear or cleverly stated that people will immediately stop being cognitive misers and absorb it, magically.

That assumption is wrong. In this experiment messages worked better when they worked *with* people's expectations. Better communication is achieved when we *don't* make people stop and think. Messages should steer people along the route they were already on without interrupting them.

The cognitive model of behaviour change rests on an assumption that we are rational beings analysing the incentives offered to us, and that people are best influenced by more information to change our minds. What behavioural economics teaches us is that automatic processes affect the way we respond to our environment (the 'context' model). It is not information, but the *context* within which people act that is important. We are more often guided by instinctive mental shortcuts (heuristics) than logic or reflective decision-making.

The research evidenced that physically rich, tangible objects open our minds to brands, ideas, messages and values. Our view is that objects *prime* messages making people more receptive to them, and that more tangible objects deliver stronger primes[11][12].

Research outcomes

There were several key research outcomes.

A new argument for how mail works

The research was used as a conceptual tool to assist advertisers using mail in their integrated campaigns. The message was positive: using mail means you have got another dimension to explore when planning a campaign – capitalizing on our sense of touch.

FIGURE 6.11   Challenging advertisers about what makes advertising mail successful

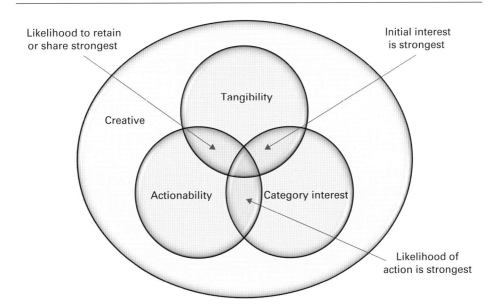

Production in context

The model notes the importance of tangibility, but places it in context. Tangibility (eg having relevant physical effects like die cutting) is one of the four cornerstones of an effective mail piece – alongside the creative, its actionability (eg having a voucher) and category interest.

A challenge to the creative value chain

The model provides an impetus for production, creative, client and planning departments to work together. Ensuring these four cornerstones are correctly in place can dramatically increase response rates: this is vital information when investing in a mail campaign.

The optimum role for physical media within the media mix

The research facilitated Royal Mail with a single-minded story to tell about mails' strengths:

- Physical media is good at generating emotional responses.

- Print can make ideas *more* substantial. Messages are secondary to the medium: the physical form tells the story. Intrinsic qualities signal values.

- As physical communications are becoming rarer in our digital world, physically rich printed objects possess greater standout and power.

Research impact

Results from both case studies formed a substantial element of an in-depth research report – *The Private Life of Mail*.[13] In February 2015 MarketReach launched the *Mail Men* campaign which again drew on the research findings. *Mail Men* generated an unprecedented level of interest in mail:

- The campaign generated 22,534 unique visitors to the campaign site (**www.mailmen. co.uk**) equivalent to a 56 per cent engagement rate.

- Twitter activity performed exceptionally well breaking the industry benchmark engagement rate by over 300 per cent in the campaign's second week (benchmark 1 to 3 per cent vs. 10.8 per cent).

- 53 per cent of agencies said that the campaign made them think differently about mail.

- There was a 30 per cent increase in advertisers saying they were likely to use mail in the next 12 months.

- Mail volumes increased by 5 per cent over the campaign period.

  'We're very excited about this research, which has uncovered an entirely new perspective on mail's effectiveness and made a clear and compelling argument for its continued place in the 21st century media mix. It's certainly made us think differently about mail, and we genuinely believe it will do the same for the industry as a whole.'

                                                  Mike Welsh, CEO of Publicis Chemistry

FIGURE 6.12 London Underground executions for the Mailmen campaign

Using behavioural economic thinking in advertising and media research

1 In our project, mail was working in ways we couldn't evidence through traditional methods. People couldn't tell us the answer, so we had to examine their behaviour (observation and biometric measurement).

2 We relied on experimental design to isolate what we were interested in. Controlled experiments enable firm conclusions and actionable rules, but rely on keeping all variables the same and changing just one. We had to be sure that we were only looking at the effects of tangibility and not existing brand perceptions, hence the production of fake brands.

3 Secondary research was our starting point: randomized controlled trials provided inspiration for research design.

4 We collaborated, learning from whoever had a good idea. We engaged with neuroscience specialists to deliver the biometric elements. Their expertise assisted experimental design (order effects and stimulus presentation) and data interpretation.

5 When you receive your client brief, consider the root causes of media effects. In our example there was misattribution over the channel and production.

6 Had we conducted the experiment for a client, rather than a media owner, we would have extended the study into a large test/control campaign, using two versions of the same campaign materials, making an effort to control for confounding factors.

7 Make a virtue of naturally occurring controlled experiments. For example, a geographical variation in distribution ('We are only in 3 of the big 4 retailers'). Double-check for confounding factors (eg a sale or promotion) and investigate.

References

1 The TV advertising industry body thinkbox commissioned econometric modelling to examine the direct and indirect effects of different media: https://www. thinkbox.tv/Getting-on-TV/Planning-and-Buying-TV/TV-and-other-media

2 Les Binet and Sarah Carter provide a detailed analysis of the issues in the WARC blog entitled *Attribution Fraud*: www.warc.com/Blogs/Mythbuster_ Attribution_fraud.blog?ID=2227

3 www.royalmail.com/business/insights/how-to-guides/building-a-business-case

4 www.aqr.org.uk/glossary/ethnography

5 Gold, R. 1958. Roles in Sociological Field Observation. *Social Forces* 36 (3): 217–223.

6 See the interview with Danny Miller in Ethnography Matters: http:// ethnographymatters.net/blog/2014/02/12/an-interview-with-anthropologist-danny-miller-about-his-latest-research-on-social-media-hospices/

7 See Gillian Thomas' Anthropology webinar on the AQR website: www.aqr.org.uk/events/thehub/webinar.shtml?w=20160127

8 Sharp, B: *How Brands Grow: What Marketers Don't Know.* Oxford University Press, 2010. ISBN-10: 0195573560

9 McLuhan, M: Understanding Media: The Extensions of Man. New American Library, 1964. ISBN: 81-14-67535-7

10 Sharp, B: *How Brands Grow: What Marketers Don't Know.* Oxford University Press, 2010. ISBN-10: 0195573560

11 Supporting evidence comes from research by Neuro-Insight for Royal Mail in 2013 using Steady State Topography (SST), which showed a strong, universal response to mail when directly measuring brain response. Engagement, emotional intensity and long-term memory encoding were superior for mail than email or TV (see Royal Mail MarketReach, *Neuro-Insight*, 2013, p27 in http://mailmen.co.uk/campaigns/the-private-life-of-mail).

12 In experiments, people value something 24 per cent more highly when they can see and touch it, compared to only seeing it (Peck, Joann, and Suzanne B. Shu. The Effect of Mere Touch on Perceived Ownership. *Journal of Consumer Research*, 2009).

13 http://mailmen.co.uk/campaigns/the-private-life-of-mail

Blueprint research

07

W hen Jungle Green undertook a project to assist Northern Railway to strengthen its community rail partnerships, it discovered the power of taking a direct approach. Janice Guy explains how.

FIGURE 7.1   Northern Rail Community Ambassadors

The business need

In 2004 Serco and Abellio won the franchise to run train services across the North of England and formed Northern Rail. Over time, a 'Northern' culture became established, which is reflected in Northern Rail's values and actions. This culture is formed around a desire to deliver local railway services that the North can be proud of and that really work for everyone.

A key element of Northern's culture is a strong focus on community rail. For example, Northern recognize the value of the work of Community Rail Partnerships (CRPs) and currently sponsor 18 CRPs, more than any other train operating company. These CRPs work to bring together the railways and the local communities. Their work includes bringing station buildings back to life, art and education projects and organizing special events which promote the railway and its relevance to the community.

Building on this community focus, Northern wished to set up a Community Ambassadors' Scheme to promote the use of rail services with Black and Minority Ethnic (BME) and socially excluded groups on their network. It was to be modelled on a concept developed earlier by Serco on Docklands Light Railway, based in London.

Northern hoped that a fresh, more direct approach would attract new users onto the railway and help them to build positive relationships with communities where traditional marketing had made little impact.

To understand the barriers these potential new rail users faced, Northern recruited Ambassadors who had strong links with the targeted areas. They also commissioned Jungle Green to conduct a significant programme of research activity running throughout the pilot period of the scheme. Through the Ambassadors' knowledge and hard work, coupled with the detailed feedback from the research programme, Northern were able to support people and break down perceived barriers to travel. In some cases their work also led to increased footfall at the local stations and, even more importantly, a legacy of train use has been built which will continue for years to come.

The following chapter explains how the scheme and the research were approached, the lessons that were learned along the way and the real difference that has been made to the people who have taken part. Northern are immensely proud of what the Ambassadors have achieved.

Setting up the scheme

The Northern Rail Community Ambassadors' scheme was created to promote the use of local rail services within BME and socially excluded groups on the network. Initially, this focused on four locations in the North West: Blackburn, Brierfield, Rochdale and Farnworth. These locations were selected as the population profile included a high proportion of the target groups.

Together with Northern's colleagues at the Department for Transport (DfT), Transport for Greater Manchester and the East Lancashire Community Rail Partnership, they wanted to understand and then break down the barriers to rail travel.

Moving away from their normal recruitment process, Northern conducted a mail-drop in the relevant locations and used posters in local shops and community centres to attract people from within the communities. Following this process, four part-time Ambassadors (working 16 hours per week) were recruited to join the full-time Project Manager.

To help the scheme gain momentum, Ambassadors with strong local knowledge and existing relationships within the targeted communities were recruited. Excellent communication skills were also essential and so, to overcome the language barrier, Northern recruited a team of people who were fluent in Punjabi, Urdu and Hindi.

Aims of the scheme

With the support of their funding partners, Northern hoped that the scheme would:

- Increase the use of local rail services at the target locations.
- Help them to build positive relationships with the local communities.
- Provide a blueprint to help other organizations engage with BME and socially excluded communities.

The scheme in action

On a day-to-day basis, the Ambassadors were involved in a range of activities, such as visiting community and faith centres, giving talks to local groups and organizing group accessibility trips to show people how easy it is to use rail services. The Ambassadors deliberately targeted a wide range of people, including the elderly, job clubs and colleges. Where English was not the first language, the trips were often conducted in Urdu or Punjabi and they were tailored to each group, taking them to a local destination which they would find interesting or useful.

Blueprint research project

The research brief was clear in setting out the business needs and research evaluation objectives:

> Despite serving areas of high multi-ethnic communities, Northern had yet to engage in any systematic way with socially-excluded ethnic minority communities, and indeed some socially excluded indigenous white communities. If Northern were better able to engage with these communities they believed there would be benefits in terms of revenue and ridership growth, reduced anti-social behaviour and stronger stakeholder relationships with groups representing ethnic communities.

There were several dimensions to a successful outcome for the Northern ambassadors.

Crucially, Northern wanted to see:

- clear evidence of greater use of each station by members of the target communities;
- quantified evidence of improved customer satisfaction with Northern Rail at the target locations;
- active involvement of the local communities targeted, through station partnerships and community rail partnerships;
- reductions in crime and vandalism at the target stations;
- endorsement and support from local authorities and Department for Transport (DfT);
- positive local media coverage;
- winning of awards for a highly innovative project.

The aim of the research evaluation study was to provide Northern with transferable lessons about whether the ambassador pilot and specific elements of it had worked or not and why. The objectives of the evaluation research were to:

- Evaluate the extent to which the Northern pilot community ambassador initiative was being delivered/operated in the way it was designed to operate (process evaluation).

- Evaluate the extent to which the Northern pilot community ambassador initiative was meeting its objectives eg in terms of increasing station passenger throughput by the targeted local community (impact evaluation).

- Identify the factors driving success.

- Identify the factors hindering success.

- Based on the evidence from across the pilot areas, identify what types of ambassador interventions were most and least successful and why; what transferable lessons about the design and delivery of a successful community ambassador scheme could be drawn from across the pilot areas and could be applied to other similar areas.

As the evaluation research ran largely in parallel with the 12-month pilot, the research was to focus initially on gathering relevant baseline data. The data was to be used to influence how the pilot ambassadors worked in their particular locations. Towards the end of the pilot, Northern expected there to be some evidence of what was or was not working and the researchers were expected to obtain and analyse relevant data and undertake surveys of local residents as required. The results from this data analysis and further surveys were to inform the final report and transferable lessons.

The ultimate aim of the extensive research programme, running alongside the pilot phase of the Ambassadors' scheme, was to help Northern and their partners to create a Community Ambassador Scheme blueprint that could be replicated by or provide valuable transferable lessons for other transport operators or similar organizations wishing to introduce such a scheme.

Jungle Green as a research partner

Northern were looking for a research partner with whom they could work very closely and one that they could trust to conduct the research in a sensitive, professional, efficient and highly effective manner. The scale of the project clearly required competitive tendering and Jungle Green was delighted to be successful in being awarded the project.

Jungle Green and Northern had conducted many research projects together since 2006. This wide experience of the network and the partners involved enabled the research company to understand the context of the project in some depth and to design a varied and creative programme of research activity.

Research scope

The research clearly needed to be conducted on the ground in the specific communities, face to face, with translators where necessary. There was a need for both quantitative research to measure impact and qualitative research to gain a deep understanding of the needs, feelings and behaviours of the targeted groups.

A number of personal case studies were also prepared to bring the research findings to life.

Quantitative research

During the early months of the pilot scheme, initial quantitative research was carried out to set a baseline to measure against and to provide Ambassadors with information to aid in their work. A sample of residents, representative of the population profile in each of the targeted areas, was interviewed. Key sample points (usually busy high streets and market areas with proximity to local community facilities) within each community were selected and a shift pattern was carefully programmed to cover weekdays, weekends and early mornings through to late evenings. The sample points, profiles and shift pattern were all to be repeated exactly in the follow-up research.

Early research

The early research focused on current feelings and behaviours relating to the use or non-use of the local rail network. This included rail awareness, process knowledge, any current or past rail usage, perceived barriers to rail usage and ideas on how these barriers could be reduced. There were also questions on the use of other modes of transport.

FIGURE 7.2   Jungle Green quantitative research in the early stages of the pilot scheme, January 2011

Ambassadors Scheme – early quant feedback

One in 20 non rail users do not know where the local railway station is and many say that access is not that easy, especially BME participants. Some suggestions for making access easier and for making local rail use more attractive and better value for money were:

- More shelter
- Improved access for disabled, prams
- Better lighting
- Modernisation
- Shuttle bus to/from station
- Multi language instructions
- More advertising, publicity
- Better signage
- More awareness of how to use rail & stations and what to do
- Better weekend service

- Family tickets
- Cheaper for children
- Special offers
- Cheaper fares for disabled, OAP's, students, unemployed
- Pointing out VFM compared to rising petrol prices
- Cheaper at weekends
- Cheaper after 9.30
- Weekly tickets
- More awareness of fares, timetables etc.
- All inclusive trips to venues, events etc.

jungle green

Quantitative research insights

Many of the people encountered in the research had little or no experience of using rail services and they believed them to be expensive, complicated, unreliable and unsafe (particularly for females). It was interesting to note that those who held these concerns were those with the least experience of actually using the local rail services. The views they held were based on their *perceptions* of what using a rail service would be like, rather than any direct experience. This made it clear, very early on in the pilot, that helping people in these communities to experience the rail service would enable them to form opinions based on reality rather than perception.

Addressing concerns

Accessibility trips facilitated by the Ambassadors had the potential to change perceptions through real experience. The Ambassadors worked hard to overcome the negative perceptions and found that reassurance could be provided by simple acts, such as providing examples of journey opportunities and prices. Similarly, on the safety question, people felt much more confident once the

CCTV cameras were pointed out to them and they understood that they could contact the conductor if they were concerned during their journey. Explanation of group ticketing, off-peak travel and other fare offers informed the communities on cheaper ways to travel.

At the end of the pilot scheme time period in February 2012, 12 months after the initial quantitative research was undertaken, the quantitative research programme was repeated and measures of impact were thus produced.

Impact results

FIGURE 7.3   Jungle Green quantitative research at the end of the pilot scheme. February 2012

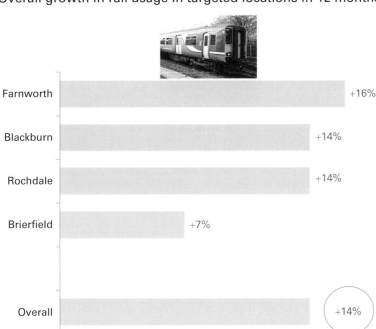

Overall growth in rail usage in targeted locations in 12 months

Farnworth	+16%
Blackburn	+14%
Rochdale	+14%
Brierfield	+7%
Overall	+14%

It was clear that the Ambassadors' Scheme was having significant impact. This was backed up by evidence of increased ticket sales in these locations.

The follow-up research found that:

- There had been overall growth in rail usage at the targeted locations of around 14 per cent; approximately half of this growth could be directly attributed to the Ambassadors.

- These new users had mainly come from certain sectors of the community, ie mainly C2DE social grades (eg skilled and unskilled manual workers and those who rely on the welfare state for their income), mainly females, from BME communities who were infrequent travellers.

- The vast majority of those who had been on an accessibility trip said that they were now finding it easier to use trains (83 per cent) and over half of them (54 per cent) were already using the train independently.
- Northern brand awareness had increased, by 20 per cent in one location, and reputation had been enhanced. The scheme had a significant impact in particular on perceptions of having helpful employees, running reliable services and offering good value fares.

Qualitative research

In addition to the quantitative research, a series of groups, mini groups, community workshops, friendship depth interviews and observations were conducted. In all cases, a representative from the specific local community involved was present, along with any necessary translators.

The Ambassadors themselves also took part in the research process so that their experiences and learnings could be included in the eventual blueprint.

Research venues and participant groups were many and varied, including:

- local community centres;
- carers' groups;
- learning disability centres;
- homes for the elderly;
- parent and toddler groups;
- Sure Start Centres;
- neighbourhood and learning centres;
- libraries;
- markets;
- Asian women's groups;
- women's refuge groups;
- Job Clubs;
- housing associations;
- walking groups;
- schools;
- church groups;
- student groups.

The primary aim of the qualitative research was to gain a greater understanding of the impact of the scheme among those exposed to it. It was evident very quickly in the qualitative research that the impact ran deep.

Qualitative research insights

The qualitative insights that emerged revealed that one of the most significant contributions that the Ambassadors' Scheme accessibility trips had made in these communities was to raise confidence levels among those with low levels of self-confidence, such as those who had suffered domestic violence, the elderly and infirm, young teenagers, single mothers and Asian women. This confidence-raising had very often led to repeated use of the train independently, which was something many of these participants would never have considered doing previously. The increased confidence levels were not only self-reported by participants but mentioned by the group/community leaders also interviewed in the qualitative research. It was also evident from the increased rail trips made.

The accessibility trips, where individuals and groups were introduced to and accompanied by an Ambassador on a rail trip, had opened participants' eyes to the relative ease with which rail trips can be made. They had broken down the negative perception barriers (identified in the early quantitative research) that rail travel was expensive, complicated, unreliable and unsafe.

Impacts of the scheme

Various impacts were seen as a direct result of the Ambassadors' scheme:

- Word of mouth in these close-knit communities was prevalent. Those who had experienced the accessibility trips were telling their friends and family and taking them with them on future trips independently.
- The social stigma of public transport among BME communities was being replaced with a view that it is for fun family trips – replacing a common view that travelling by train was a sign that no one in your family cared enough for you to drive you to where you need to go.
- Many mothers were now taking their young children on trips in the holidays, revisiting locations they had encountered on the accessibility trips and venturing to new ones too.

- Elderly people and those with disabilities had been reintroduced to rail travel. Both they and their carers were feeling more confident about using the train in the future.

- Family members and friends, who had not seen each other regularly for a long time, were being reconnected via rail travel and those seeking work had been encouraged to look further afield and travel there by train.

- The Ambassadors had become highly respected and very popular figures in the local communities in a very short time. Much of the uncertainty about rail travel had been removed for many of those who the Ambassadors engaged with.

- The scheme lessened many of the unknowns about rail travel for those with a language barrier, making this less of an issue in the future.

- Station location awareness had increased and the reputation of the rail industry improved in these neighbourhoods, especially in terms of accessibility, value for money, ease of use and caring about the community.

FIGURE 7.4   Jungle Green qualitative research at the end of the pilot scheme. February 2012

Benefits of the Ambassadors Scheme

Planting the seed of a love of rail travel for life

Getting young people to university and reassuring parents

Developing parent-child relationships through fun days out and learning experiences

Enabling those with disabilities to travel and their carers to rediscover travel

Bringing communities together and connecting people. Reducing social stigma of public transport.

Rebuilding shattered lives through connecting and confidence building

Enabling the elderly to reconnect with their families and rediscover travel

Helping people to find work further afield

Building confidence to venture out and travel further afield

Bringing the findings to life

A separate document of **People's Stories** was prepared by Jungle Green to help bring the findings to life. The following are snippets from this document, in the words of the research participants.

'I get bad panic attacks, so I've never thought I could use trains as a mother of three kids. When I found out that you could experience the train with someone who could show you all about it and would travel with you, I really wanted to give it a try. Because I've never taken my kids on the train, I really wanted to give them that experience. I could never have taken them on my own; I couldn't have managed that at all. Having the support of others in the group was really good. I never even knew that Farnworth station was there before. We've been on a few trips now on our own and our confidence is building.'
(Parent Group)

'It's been so beneficial for the women and children. Previous experience of trains for the women here is pretty non-existent and that's certainly true for the kids. They are fleeing domestic violence and they have been quite controlled and isolated so the scheme offers a lot more than experience of the trains. It's confidence building, it's a whole new freedom experience, it's promoting independence. It really helps them think about a better future. They don't have cars for a start and they are used to being controlled totally. We have a constant stream of new women coming and going through here, so there is a constant need for the scheme.' **(Women's Refuge)**

'Introducing the train travel idea to these women in here is brilliant because they go on to live independently afterwards and, instead of still feeling lonely and isolated, they have new ideas of where to take the children on trips and how to get out and about and integrate again. The women and children's relationships often suffer because of domestic violence and these trips help to rebuild those relationships. In fact it's often the first time they've done anything like it together at all.' **(Women's Refuge)**

'We were really, really scared about trains as we'd never used them before. Families just don't travel very far around here so we don't know about it. So when we saw the leaflet at the station for the Northern Ambassadors we were really interested. We got in touch with Sultana who said we could go on a trip with her to experience the trains and get used to it. It's been brilliant and we feel quite confident about going by train to university now.' **(Students)**

'I've found it most useful for people looking for work. It's opened their eyes to the possibility of working outside of Blackburn. They've learned about tickets, timetables, routes, they've had tours of the train station and it's really, really helped. Sultana comes in to some of the job clubs and helps them find all the information they need on the internet.'
(Job Club)

'In our culture we are always thinking 'Oh no, you can't use the train', but now we say 'Yes you can, of course you can'. It's just lack of awareness and just the way our culture is, but it is changing a bit now. We are very over protective of our children too. We drop them right outside the door. We need to realise that they are capable of doing things for themselves and can go by train, also that they are safe doing it. This scheme is helping in that goal too.' *(Children's Centre)*

'We have over 40 people in our group and so different people come each time we meet. Our people do not get out of the house very often and have low confidence. The language barrier is the main problem for them, along with their carer duties obviously. We've been twice to Bradford on accessibility trips with different ones and they were quite surprised at how easy it was. It takes time but they feel more confident now.' *(Carer's group)*

'Public transport is seen as a "poor" person's pursuit, even though ticket prices are quite high. The reason is cultural; children are brought up to respect their elders and look after them, so if they are seen on public transport it suggests to others that their children have no respect for them and do not look after them as they should. This is seen as a stigma in this culture.' *(Community Group)*

'Our women are now able to get on the train when they've never been able to before. They would not have even contemplated it through lack of confidence, lack of awareness, disability, mental health problems, cultural reasons and lack of ambition in life.' *(Ambassador)*

'Children having the best time they have ever had, seeing the smiles on their faces is so worth it, something they'll treasure and also planting the seed for future train travel.' *(Ambassador)*

'One lady is 97 and she just loved being on a train again. Before doing the trip with Simon I thought it would be too difficult with people in wheelchairs, but everyone was so helpful.' *(Home for the Elderly)*

Where the scheme is now

From early 2012, the scheme was jointly funded by Northern and the Citizens' Rail Interreg IVB project.

As the scheme became established, a part-time Project Manager and three Ambassadors collectively worked a total of 75 hours per week. Instead of focusing on a single location, they worked along circular lines of route between Burnley, Rochdale, Bolton and Blackburn.

In the second phase of the scheme, focus on the local student communities increased, in the hope that they continue to use the railway as they move into the world of employment.

This approach enables Northern to reach more of the BME and socially excluded communities which they serve, helping them to use local rail services and improving their access to employment, education and leisure opportunities in the region.

In December 2015 (as this chapter was being written) the Department for Transport announced Arriva as the new franchise holder for the Northern network. The new franchise period starts in April 2016 when the new franchisee will make clear plans and programmes for the future.

Arriva said in their first statement about the new franchise:

> *'Our aim is to be the communities' local railway and to leave a positive lasting legacy for the North of England.'*

The Community Ambassadors' Scheme has the evidenced scope to contribute towards this aim. Jungle Green hopes that the research and subsequent blueprint document can help the new franchisee to set out their plans for future community rail initiatives.

Award winning scheme with European recognition

In terms of wider recognition, the scheme went on to win the following awards:

- The Small Scale Project category at The Railway Industry Innovation Awards 2012;

- The Diversity and Equality category at the Civil Service Awards 2012 (working together with the Community Rail Team at the Department for Transport);

- Customer Service Excellence at the European Rail Congress Awards, Nov 2013.

Reflections on the research programme

This was, and still is, one of the most satisfying projects that the Jungle Green researchers have undertaken. The research produced a rich array of findings and more than answered the original objectives set. The researchers took away a number of insights from the project and these have proved valuable to them in their work since.

- A project of this nature requires a small dedicated team of two or three people: enough to share thoughts and cross reference but not too many to miss the benefits of deep immersion in a project.

- When referring to qualitative research, Jungle Green now always tries to use the term 'immersion days'. This helps all involved to focus on what qualitative research really is.

- The importance of ensuring that participants from all backgrounds feel comfortable enough to speak openly and candidly about their lives was clearly evident in this research. Many different venues, appropriate escorts, translators and different methods of capturing the research findings were all key considerations in this project.

- Researchers are in an extremely privileged position. Every day they have the chance to meet extraordinary people living ordinary lives, who share their thoughts and feelings on all manner of topics. Some of these topics are simply interesting and some can be fun to listen to. Others run deeper and stay with the researcher for a very long time; this project was one of those and Jungle Green actively seeks out projects of a similar nature.

- The experience on this project, and other factors, led to a number of other projects being awarded to Jungle Green by a variety of health and charitable organizations. It has also been valuable in informing the company's approach to commercial projects involving 'brands with purpose'.

- The learnings from this research piece have had wide application in Jungle Green's extensive rail research. If individuals are not habitual train users, or have not travelled by train for a long time, it is common to find that the perceptions held of what travelling on a rail network would be like centre on complexity, personal security issues, expense and unreliability. This is found to be true for people from a wide variety of backgrounds. These negative perceptions can often be transformed through the simple encouragement and incentive to take a rail journey and gain current experience.

The **final word** on our case study comes from Northern:

> the research not only identified the key quantitative measures we needed but also transferable lessons which could be used by other train operators and organizations wanting to establish a similar scheme elsewhere in the country. This covers lessons learned from establishing the scheme with community group leaders, which activities were the most and least successful and suggestions from the Ambassadors for future improvements. We have currently collated these lessons into a booklet available for all stakeholders and interested parties at www.northernrail.org

Public policy research

08

There has never been a more challenging time to work in public policy research, but it's never been more rewarding, explains Ben Page, Chief Executive of Ipsos MORI.

Introduction

In recent years public policy and social research within the UK have changed substantially. One of the most important drivers of this has, of course, been a tightening of the purse strings – government departments and other public bodies, as in many sectors, simply have less money at their disposal than before 2010. This has had a significant impact on the quality criteria used to judge public policy research; in austere times, the work we do must have a clear purpose and demonstrate real value for money while also delivering genuine insight.

This in part explains why large-scale social surveys have mostly survived austerity, though not without a fight; back in 2009, Conservative MP Nick Hurd described the Census as 'bedroom snooping' and its future is still uncertain. Nonetheless, surveys still account for a significant proportion of the public money spent on research – but away from this kind of work it is important to recognize that the public sector has many other research needs.

Social research: a changing landscape

Social research has changed quite dramatically. The scale of the public policy challenges grow ever larger, more diverse and more complex – from understanding community cohesion, responding to the pressures facing the NHS and supporting people into an increasingly flexible labour market through to encouraging people to take action on climate change.

Social changes relating to technology have had a major impact: the proliferation of new digital channels, coupled with the rise of smartphones as the main source of web access for a large proportion of the population, has changed how researchers can interact with respondents – although the demand for high quality face-to-face interviewing for data collection has continued. The way in which we as researchers respond and operate needs to evolve accordingly.

Different kinds of evidence and evaluation

The questions that we are asking as public policy researchers have adapted in line with changing government needs. In the early noughties, public policy research often focused on providing descriptive accounts. These were rich illustrations of what was going on in any given situation, which then laid the ground for policy makers to develop appropriate responses. Now, however, what matters is to establish whether what government is doing is making a difference and achieving policy aims, and what the drivers for this are. This has led to a reversal of the old order; government now uses different kinds of evidence – administrative data for instance – to develop policy but then uses its research budget to evaluate the impact of what it is doing. Such a shift of emphasis has led to and underpinned a rapid growth in the evaluation market in recent years. It has meant that researchers have had to develop new skills to cater for this demand.

New skills and strategies

Given how challenging it is to determine what works, the use of interdisciplinary and mixed methods approaches has become all the more important. Increasingly, a simple survey can no longer tell us all we need to know; instead, research studies that blend quantitative data with qualitative and ethnographic approaches are much more likely to get us closer to the answers that our public sector clients need. Complementing this, big data, behavioural science and RCTs are all increasingly part of the social researcher's tool kit – something which poses a challenge for supply-side researchers; in this kind of environment is there still a role for method specialists or, instead, should we aim to be generalists?

Behavioural science

Behavioural science – as popularized by the government's 'nudge unit' – is increasingly a key area of focus for public policy researchers. Laws can, of course, be passed to mandate certain behaviours, but much of what government wants to achieve – encouraging people to reduce their sugar intake, to drink less or to save for the future, for instance – requires a more subtle approach.

The types of behaviours that policy makers want to understand and influence may differ from those of interest to big business – but the approaches used to do so overlap. For government, finding cost effective ways to influence behaviour – from improving how we interact with public services to the kinds of lifestyles choices we make – will be increasingly important in the years ahead. As such, ensuring that we as researchers have ways to help our clients with this will matter more and more and those research suppliers who fail to adapt will be left behind in an ever more competitive market place.

Big data

Big data raises questions that government is grappling with. How can – and should – it use 'big data'? While there are some examples of individual departments using data analytics to improve policy and services, sharing and linking data across different areas of government is still relatively rare. Currently, linking data tends to focus on specific projects, where there is a clear case for making connections between data held in different places.

However, looking ahead, government will need to make difficult trade-offs. This means considering the potential benefits and risks of making better use of government data to streamline delivery and tailor services – while bearing in mind the real concerns among the public about using data in this way. This is particularly important in instances where the private sector becomes involved in high profile and sensitive areas of public policy. It will be up to us as public policy researchers to help our clients chart this unfamiliar terrain if we wish to stay ahead.

Communicating complex ideas

Running in parallel with these changes to approaches and focus, it seems that research capacity within government has dwindled; with many departmental research teams cut, there is a greater reliance on external expertise and research suppliers increasingly act as an interface between the public and policy. This changing approach has forced us to think about how we communicate complex – and often contentious – findings to an audience that may not know much about research methods, such as front-line staff delivering services, and marketing and communications teams.

Of course, the best public policy researchers have done this for years. But, more than ever, we need to be open to what we can learn from our counterparts who, in working for private sector clients, understand the art of communicating findings to a decision maker who is not interested in sampling or weighting but, instead, just wants to know what to do and what the evidence is for this. In order for public policy researchers to get better at this we need to work closely with government clients, to ensure that the recommendations we make remain grounded in evidence but are framed in a way that is compelling and makes them stick. We can do this through data visualization, story-telling techniques, film, photography, animation and immersive experiences – and these approaches can mean our research has a direct impact on key areas of public policy.

Conclusion

Taking all of these influencing factors together, the public policy research landscape is almost unrecognizable from how it has traditionally looked – and it would be foolish to think that the pace of change will let up or slow down. This means that, of course, there will be challenges ahead for us – in thinking about what we do, and our role in the public policy process. It also demands more of us. We must work more quickly, more flexibly, more collaboratively and get more out of the data that we collect, so our clients can confidently use it to inform crucial decisions about society.

These are challenging times but, equally, there has never been a more exciting time to work in this field. For one thing, the evidence we gather is being used – reports are no longer left forgotten and gathering dust on shelves in Whitehall corridors. This is surely why we do this job in the first place. What's more, as research capacity within government itself is reduced, we are now the experts. We have the licence and legitimacy to suggest more innovative and radical approaches to help address the thorny issues our public sector clients have to tackle. With such challenges in plentiful supply, it is safe to say that we can be optimistic about the future of the sector; it will continue to attract the brightest talents who recognize these challenges for what they are – a privilege which affords us the ability to make a difference.

Mapping attention in the digital era

09

Through their work with Microsoft Advertising, Sparkler challenged the received wisdom that our attention spans are reducing and instead suggest that they are evolving. Sparkler's Andy Goll explains.

The challenge

The challenges to making an effective advertising campaign are many and various. One of the first is: how do you grab a consumer's attention? And once grabbed, how do you hold and marshal attention for the best commercial results? While there are lots of research studies that measure how effectively attention has been used in specific campaigns, few market research studies go beyond this and ask questions about the nature of attention in advertising.

Attention has long been a subject of interest to academics in neuroscience and psychology as well as being a subject under constant debate as part of much marketing theory and practice. However, it is only relatively recently that anyone has gone beyond common-sense intuition and scientifically investigated attentions role and function with specific reference to advertising (Robert Heath in his book *Seducing the Subconscious* is the best example we know of this).[1]

The digital media hypothesis

Sparkler and Microsoft Advertising think that having a deeper understanding of attention in the context of advertising is increasingly important with the advent of digital and mobile technology. Both academic and mainstream journalism are hypothesizing that digital media activity is dulling our ability to attend to tasks for a prolonged period of time. Digital advertisers are responding by increasingly intertwining adverts with content and selling ads programmatically, all in the hope of overcoming a dearth of attention in the modern digital consumer.

But, taking a step back, is this really what is going on? Are our devices actually dulling our ability to pay attention or is this a myth? For many media owners the focus on ad effectiveness is paramount for their ongoing business, and so much of the research they commission is focused on the purely quantifiable metrics of clicks, views, awareness or brand response generated by a particular campaign. But approaching the study of ad effectiveness without taking into account the broader environment in which it is encountered, ignores the reciprocal relationship between our cognitive processes and the environment in which we spend our time.

Neuroscience and digital media consumption

Modern neuroscience calls the ability of our brain to change or adapt to the tasks or the environment in which we find ourselves 'neuroplasticity'. As digital media consumption grows and intensifies, the brain's neurological structure is likely to change in response, enhancing and developing certain cognitive skills to match our needs. In this way, digital media is likely to impact not just the way we consume media through mobile, tablet or a connected device but how we process, digest and think about it. If our cognitive skills are changing in response to the digital environments we increasingly inhabit, then we need to think about how that might impact advertising. It seems that the most salient cognitive skill to consider in relation to advertising is attention.

The brief

Microsoft Advertising wanted us to explore the link between digital media and attention to see if there were any quantifiable shifts in attention, if any of these shifts were associated with digital media usage and what impact these shifts might they be having.

The project was therefore about broadening and driving the debate around the link between digital devices and attention. Microsoft Advertising also wanted us to try and apply whatever we found to the digital advertising context, informing Microsoft Advertising and their clients about how best to adapt and improve digital advertising to make better use of attention.

To achieve these objectives, we needed to answer three key questions:

1 How are attention spans evolving in the connected digital world?

2 How does evolving attention impact on what we do and how we do it?

3 What does this mean for media and advertising agencies?

Microsoft Advertising was interested in understanding attention from a variety of perspectives. They wanted us to develop a methodology that could quantitatively measure people's attention and detect shifts in a comparable way, so that we could compare groups of consumers (eg mums and millennials) that were particularly important to their clients. It was also important that this wasn't just a quantitative piece; we needed to pick up the nuance and qualitative texture around attention in a way that could be linked to the quantitative phase and breathe life into the numbers.

The approach

The biggest challenge for the study was how best to measure attention. We wanted to develop a metric that was scalable across a large sample, so we could compare across demographic groupings, but that also could be somehow linked to ethnographic observation of the consumer's real-life behaviour.

To begin with, we conducted an audit of academic literature on attention and found a framework developed by Sohlberg and Mateer (cited in Bennett et al. 1998[2]). This model was developed to chart the recovery of patients from brain injury and split attention into a number of separate and distinct skills:

1 **Sustained attention:** maintain focus for a prolonged period of time.

2 **Selective attention:** maintain focus in the face of distraction.

3 **Alternating attention:** quickly shift focus between tasks demanding different cognitive skills.

This model is suited to our needs because while focusing for a prolonged period (what we refer to as Sustained Attention) was an aspect of attention we wished to measure, we felt that the attention skills extended beyond just this. Attention was no longer only about the ability to focus on one thing, it was equally about blocking out distractions and switching efficiently between tasks. Having a model that reflected the range of skills required in our fast-paced digital world was an important foundation. Our model needed to reflect modern life.

Methodology

Although we had a sound theoretical basis for our study, we still lacked a methodology that could reliably collect data on the different aspects of attention. We knew that we couldn't rely on consumers self-reporting their behaviours; we needed a more direct way to measure attention. Although there were tests already developed for each of these aspects of attention, they were designed for the laboratory and were not engaging or applicable to an online survey.

Therefore, we re-conceptualized the lab tests as fun and engaging games that we could integrate into an online survey environment. That way, we could collect reliable measures of the different elements of attention and maintain consumer engagement.

The games

Our games are summarized in the diagram below. Each game tested a different attention skill.

FIGURE 9.1   The games we used to capture people's different attention skills

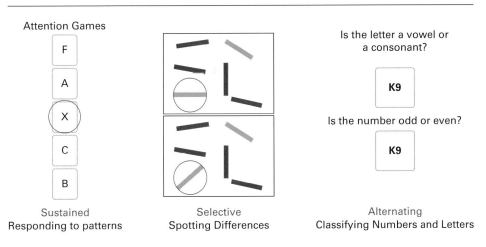

Attention Games		
Sustained	Selective	Alternating
Responding to patterns	Spotting Differences	Classifying Numbers and Letters

Is the letter a vowel or a consonant?

Is the number odd or even?

For Sustained Attention (the ability to focus for prolonged periods of time): participants were shown individual letters one after another and asked to respond every time they saw a letter X proceeded by an A. To calculate participants' levels of Sustained Attention we calculated the number of times they correctly identified an X preceded by an A.

For Selective Attention (the ability to focus in the face of distraction): sets of red and yellow rectangles were flashed up on a screen for no longer than a couple of milliseconds at a time, participants had to spot when there were changes in the position of the yellow rectangles while ignoring any movement in the red rectangles. To calculate participants' levels of Selective Attention we counted how many times they correctly identified the yellow rectangles changing position.

For Alternating Attention (the ability to move efficiently between cognitively different tasks): participants were shown a letter and a number at the same time and asked to alternate between classifying the number or letter. To calculate participants' levels of Alternating Attention we measured the average time it took for participants to carry out two similar tasks consecutively, eg classifying two numbers or two letters. We then compared that to the average time participants took to carry out two cognitively different tasks, eg classifying a number then a letter. The difference in time taken was a measure of their Alternating Attention.

Online survey and ethnographic observations

These three games were integrated into an online survey of 2000 nationally representative participants that also captured a range of data on our consumers' digital habits, lifestyles and media consumption. We mapped people's attention skills onto this lifestyle data to establish what aspects of consumers' lives were contributing to shifts in attention.

While the online survey would give us robust measures of attention, and a way to link them to differences in media consumption and lifestyle, we also wanted to conduct ethnographic observations to bring any quantitative findings to life. The challenge was: how could we apply the attention skill framework we had developed for the quantitative element to our ethnographic observations in the messy reality of everyday life?

Our solution was to use the attention tests we developed for the quantitative element to gauge the attention skills of five individuals. We then observed these five individuals as they went about their daily routines, with the knowledge gleaned from the attention tests about what sorts of attention skills they were strongest in. If a person exhibited strength in a particular attention then their behaviours, views and attitudes could be tied directly to that attention type and compared against individuals with weaknesses in the same area.

In total we spent three hours with each of these individuals. During this time we conducted the psychological tests, undertook an observed period of digital media usage for two hours, and carried out an in-depth interview about their lifestyle and digital habits structured around their views and attitudes toward their attention. We conducted in-home visits with four of the five respondents and one we visited at his office to try and get a sense of how attention played out in work as well.

By dovetailing the two elements of the methodology, our findings provided the broader cultural insight on how attention skills had shifted in response to media consumption and other lifestyle factors. In addition we gained a window into the world of five individuals so we could see how this played out in real-life. From these insights we could start to unpick what any shift in attention might mean for the digital advertisers and Microsoft Advertising's clients.

The findings

Our findings fit into two categories: first, broader cultural insights that relate to how consumers are changing to cope with the evolving media landscape; secondly, more business-focused recommendations that relate to the challenges that this shift in attention presents for digital advertisers.

Cultural nsight

The digital world is clearly having a big impact on the evolution of attention – we are making increasing use of our selective and alternating attentions in a multi-screen world. Our data reflected this, showing that while some elements of attention were strengthening with certain types of media consumption others were weakening.

1 *High volume media consumption is linked to improvements in Alternating and reductions in Sustained and Selective Attention.*

If we take in the first instance, the total volume of media consumed; for this we considered three types of media consumption: TV viewing, web browsing and gaming. The data suggested a link between Sustained and Selective Attention skills, diminishing with heavier patterns of consumption. Conversely, stronger Alternating Attention was correlated with higher volumes of media consumed. An exception to this rule was gaming; this showed a link with improvements in Selective Attention, if moderate amounts were consumed. See Figures 9.1 to 9.4.

FIGURE 9.2 Sustained attention diminishes with higher volumes of digital media consumption

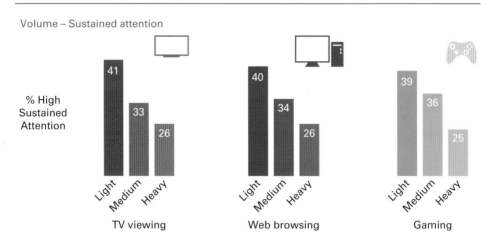

FIGURE 9.3 Selective attention diminishing with increasing volumes of digital media consumption

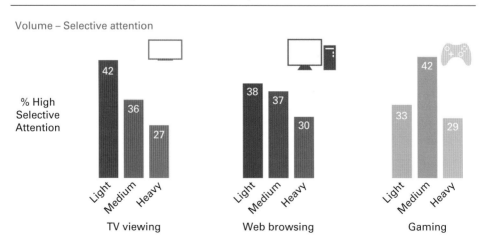

FIGURE 9.4   Alternating attention strengthens with increases in volume of consumption

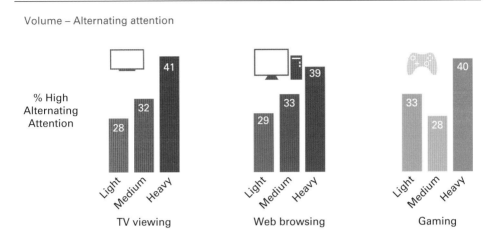

2 Multi-screening activity is linked to improvements in Alternating Attention and diminishing Sustained Attention.

We saw a similar but slightly different pattern when we considered how people were consuming media, specifically how often they were multi-screening. Multi-screening was particularly interesting because it was the sort of behaviour that might exercise particular aspects of attention, particularly Selective and Alternating Attention. What we found was that Sustained Attention was seen to diminish as multi-screening intensified, Selective Attention remained unchanged unless participants were multi-screening heavily and Alternating Attention was seen to improve as multi-screening intensified. See Figures 9.5–9.7.

FIGURE 9.5   Sustained attention diminishes as multi-screening intensifies

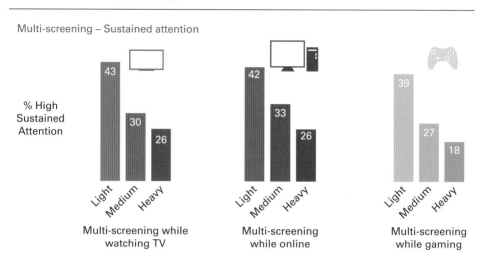

FIGURE 9.6   Selective attention remains unchanged unless respondents multi-screen intensively

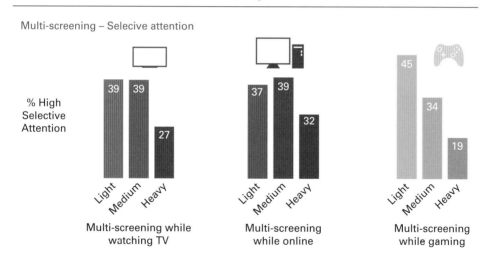

FIGURE 9.7 Alternating attention strengthens as multi-screening intensifies

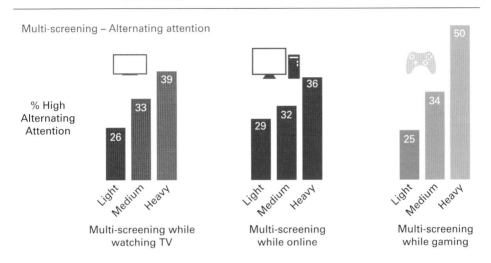

The topline findings showed some elements of our attention skills being strengthened to cope with the digital environment while others diminished. In this sense, rather than seeing our ability to pay attention as dwindling, we can instead think of it as evolving to suit our digital habits and patterns of media consumption.

3 *Younger consumers exhibit stronger Selective Attention, older consumers have stronger Alternating Attention.*

Of course not everyone has the same patterns of consumption. Microsoft Advertising tasked us specifically to investigate the differences within certain consumer groups; the most significant difference we saw was a divergence in the types of attention skills exhibited by differently aged consumers.

FIGURE 9.8 Younger consumers are more likely to be strong in terms of selective attention

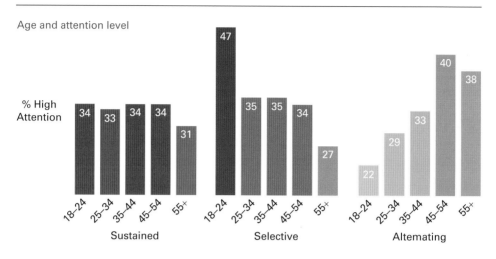

We hypothesized that the reason for this difference in attention is because the attention skills needed for the multi-screening activity each age group carries out are different. If we look at TV multi-screening, younger people are more likely than older consumers to engage in communicative multi-screening activity (see Figure 9.9), this requires the ability to block out distractions because creating and managing messages in this manner is much more attention-intensive. Older generations were more likely to use alternating attention to navigate juggling multiple media devices because the activities they do require less intensive focus to complete and therefore need less selective attention.

FIGURE 9.9 Younger people are more likely to do multi-screening activities that require them to block out distractions

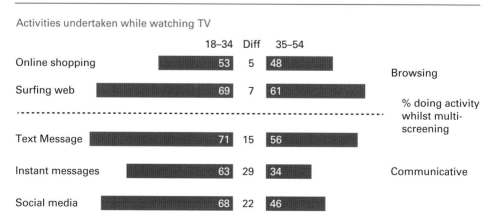

At a topline level, we saw significant shifts in attention skills where consumers' digital media consumption was markedly different. Consumers are, in effect, training their brain or evolving their attention skills in different directions by undertaking different activities.

Attention personas

In recognition of this, and as part of the findings, we created some attention personas. These personas were both derived from the quantitative data and informed by the ethnographies, and they segmented people into different groups based on their attention skills. We called these personas, attention modes. The aim was to take the more scientific and esoteric findings of the quantitative data and merge them with the ethnographic findings to give people an understanding of what the different attention skills would mean in terms of real-life behaviour (see Figure 9.10).

A caveat

These personas come with one caveat: while we are able to characterize people by their attention skills, we are not suggesting that people are completely straitjacketed by their current skill-set. If people are required to do something, or

FIGURE 9.10   Attention personas

Ninja mode - high degree of focus and compartmentalisation of tasks and devices, resistant to moving away from their current task.
Advertising Suggestion - out of the ordinary or well targeted so they will be prepared to stop what they are doing and take notice.

Pragmatist mode - comfortable switching, they are good at prioritising so will quickly move away from content that isn't suiting their needs at that moment in time.
Advertising Suggestion - be engaging, entertaining and if possible interactive to ensure that engagement is maximised.

Ambidextrous mode - move effortlessly between devices, they engage with information from a variety of sources to enhance their enjoyment or productivity.
Advertising Suggestion - be short, to the point and cross-platform so that they encounter it on a variety of devices and in a variety of contexts.

properly incentivized, they can do things unsuited to their current abilities and, if similar activities are regularly carried out, their attention skills will adapt and change to fit their new lifestyle. An example of this is a shift in job role or in your family situation, for example having children. Having children necessitates a massive lifestyle change – one that you are hopefully motivated to make. Although you might not previously have had to juggle a number of activities while looking after your children, the fact that you now *have to* juggle activities means that your attention skills will adapt and change to match your new lifestyle.

Consumers are sorted into the different attention modes based on their levels of Selective or Alternating attention – it was these skills that were seen to be most differentiating among the sample. The three modes sit across a spectrum of these skills, with Attention Ninjas being the most heavily selectively attentive while the Attention Ambidextrous are the most heavily alternating. Using this set of modes as a starting point, we could use our methodology to start to place consumers into segments based on their likely attention skills and suggest ways that advertising could be structured or presented to appeal more to them.

Business recommendations

The impact of the cultural insights uncovered in the project is hugely important for both Microsoft and its clients' approach to digital advertising, both now and in the future.

People's attention skills are adapting to better suit the digital media environments in which they spend their time and this is likely to impact on the way they process and interpret digital advertising. Understanding a group's strengths and weaknesses, and adapting the campaign to better suit their attention skills, is likely to increase a digital campaign's impact.

This adaptation is particularly apparent in younger consumers, who are exhibiting significantly higher levels of Selective Attention because of their patterns of digital media usage. As a result they are more able to block out distractions, such as adverts, and therefore it is particularly important for advertisers targeting millennials to focus on producing extraordinary, surprising and above all interactive content to cut through and get noticed.

Although some of our findings suggest consumers are setting up barriers to engagement, other findings point to the development of attention skills that can be exploited by digital advertisers. Consumers are training their attention to handle multi-screen environments; therefore agencies too must shift their approach to engaging audiences across multiple devices. Agencies can be more adventurous with their cross-platform campaigns, as consumers with Alternating Attention will have no difficulty in picking up the same stories across different devices, platforms and contexts.

The outcome

In response to the research, Microsoft has made strategic recommendations, which are already prompting advertisers and media planners to fundamentally re-appraise their approach to engaging certain groups. Furthermore, Microsoft is recommending investment in technologies, data and tools, such as programmatic advertising that allows the customization of ad execution delivery; this means they can reach audiences, at the right moment, with the right creative, on the right device – so the advertising matches their attention mode.

To provide Microsoft with a launch pad to drive conversations around attention we created a website that told the story of the research: from theoretical framework, through methodological challenges and ending with results, attention personas and business implications. We also included an attention game to engage users in the experience of the research and as a showcase of how attention should be exercised to commercial effect in the digital era. You can access the website here: **http://advertising.microsoft.com/en/attention-spans**

Since the research was launched in May, Microsoft has presented it to the likes of Nestlé, Unilever, Coca-Cola, Johnson & Johnson and Proctor & Gamble. It is working with them to ensure that the discussion of consumers' attention personas is central to ongoing marketing strategies.

The research findings have been propelled by ongoing coverage in industry publications such as *Campaign Brand Republic*, *Marketing*, *GuardianMedia Network* and *Media Week*. They have been picked up by the mainstream media including the *Daily Mail* and *Huffington Post*. The findings were also a topic of discussion on BBC Radio 5 Live which requested an interview from Microsoft to discuss how technology habits are changing people's attention.

Challenging received wisdom

In this project we challenged the received wisdom that we are experiencing a degradation of attention in the face of intensive digital media consumption. Challenging this convention involved finding ways to measure something as esoteric as attention and connecting differences in attention to real-life behaviour. As advanced analytics become increasingly able to answer questions that traditionally would have been the territory of quantitative surveys or focus groups, so market research will be asked to investigate topics such as attention that requires blending of methodological approaches. These methodological approaches that move beyond behavioural, claimed or reported data challenge us as researchers to innovate. They challenge us to build new skills, work with new people and use thinking from fields previously unrelated to market research.

What next?

We need to think carefully about the digital era and its impact on consumer behaviour, but we also need to consider what it means for market research and the new questions we are likely to get asked by our clients. What can we offer that is different from other disciplines such as data science? How can we enrich the picture that they offer? How can we work with them to build better tools to support commercial objectives?

The next step for this attention study could be to build an algorithm to identify what sort of attention users have. We could identify a sub-set of people with different attention types using our attention games and then follow their browsing activity over the course of a number of months. We could pinpoint key behaviours that identify them as having a particular attention persona, such as switching between applications or doing multiple activities at the same time. Then with the help of data scientists we could build an algorithm to identify people's attention personas based on these digital behavioural indicators rather than using our attention games. This algorithm could be integrated into web services and apps to customize how ads are shown, depending on the type of attention that users have.

References

1   Heath, R. 2012, *Seducing the Subconscious: The Psychology of Emotional Influence in Advertising*, John Wiley and Sons
2   Bennett et al. 1998, 'Rehabilitation of Attention and Concentration Deficits following Brain Injury', *Journal of Cognitive Rehabilitation*.

Digital world and private lives

10

In this chapter, Dr Michelle Goddard and Debrah Harding of MRS review the current data and privacy landscape, the legislation which affects data and the impact it has on research, and an MRS initiative, Fair Data, which has been established to retain and regain trust in the data world.

The data landscape

Data has always been gathered on individuals. In the past, the issue was the relative scarcity of data. Today, technology has liberated the collection of data to such an extent that data is now collected on a continuous basis for most aspects of our lives. This takes place via wearables, phones, cameras and, with the Internet of Things, can happen using almost any conceivable device.

To offer some context, 90 per cent of the world's data was created in the last two years.[1] An estimated 2.5 quintillion bytes of data are being generated every day and it is estimated that, by 2020, 40 zettabytes of data will have been created, a scale so large as to be almost unimaginable.[2]

Developing in tandem with this has been a huge sea change in the way such data is held and distributed. Data is no longer necessarily held within the confines of any specific organization's mainframe or a country's borders. Instead the data cloud is the reality for digital data collection, processing and transfer.

The 'quantified self'

Significant amounts of data collected are non-personal data, such as financial and environmental data and so on. But a significant part of this growth is in personal data, as a result of increasing amounts of data being captured from and about individuals.

Some of this is as a result of purposeful participation by individuals in activities such as social media. In 2015, it was estimated that there were over 2.206 billion active social media users, a global penetration of over 30 per cent.[3] Facebook alone had 1.59 billion monthly active users.[4]

However, it is not just social media activity which is generating the data about individuals. There is also the emergence of the 'Quantified Self': individuals engaged in a variety of physical, biological, environmental or behavioural activities where data is acquired from individuals through technology such as wearables, or portable devices, mobile apps and so on. Want to track physical activity, heart rate, happiness, mood, food consumption, travel, the amount being quantified? No problem, there is an app somewhere that can do this.

Risks and threats

With so much data being generated, the risks and potential for harm inexorably increases. Data scandals have been a common feature of the last few years, although the nature of these is evolving. Data losses and cyber-attacks are still very much in evidence, with an estimated 5.1 million incidents of fraud identified in the UK in 2015.[5] Organizations that are being hacked no longer just suffer the embarrassment of the publicity of being breached, often they are also being held to 'ransom' with their data as the 'captive'. Sony Pictures, TalkTalk, Ashley Madison and Domino's Pizzas were the unlucky recipients of these kinds of proposed 'trades'. It is not just big business that is suffering; in a recent study by KPMG, 60 per cent of small businesses that were surveyed had experienced a cyber breach of some sort.[6]

These data developments do not operate in a vacuum and, with increasing awareness of 'Big Data', the rise of data hacking and data abuse, inevitably individuals' views on data usage and privacy concerns are also evolving.

The privacy landscape

Data usage and privacy is a global issue of increasing concern to citizens. The Data Protection Eurobarometer study, conducted among the European Member

States, tracks attitudes of European citizens to data issues.[7] The 2015 study reported that trust in the digital environment continues to be low, with 67 per cent of participants stating they were worried about having no control over the information they provide online, while only 15 per cent feel they have complete control. Furthermore, 63 per cent of participants stated they do not trust online businesses and 62 per cent did not trust telephone and internet service providers.

These findings are replicated elsewhere around the globe. The Global Research Business Network (GRBN) Trust & Personal Data Study 2014 supported these findings, with 36 per cent of all participants expressing high levels of concern and 45 per cent fairly concerned about how personal data is collected and used. [8]

The value of data

With this increasing concern comes increasing awareness and with it the realization by individuals of the ability to leverage value from personal data, and to make much more nuanced decisions and data trades. A 2014 study by Orange, *The Future of Digital Trust*, identified that consumers attribute a value of approximately €15 to an individual piece of data with a brand they know.[9] This increases to approximately €19 for unfamiliar organizations. In this study, 80 per cent of participants knew their data had value for business and 67 per cent of participants believed that organizations benefited the most from the sharing of data. Studies such as this highlight the changing nature of the data relationship and the increasing tension that exists between those who provide data and those who use data, and the need to create an environment for a more balanced social contract.

But how can this situation be addressed? Legislation is one way to address the social contract (the 'stick' approach). An increasing number of countries are enacting some form of data protection and privacy legislation, and more are considering introducing it, as citizens become more aware of the dangers as well as the opportunities of 21st-century technology. One of the most significant developments is the new General Data Protection Regulation (GDPR), which is currently being finalized in Europe.

The legislative landscape

The finalization of the GDPR represents the culmination of the modernization of the data protection framework across the European Union (EU). Driven by dual imperatives, of giving individuals control of their data and a desire to simplify the regulatory environment for businesses, the new legislation is expected to come into force in all member states of the EU in the second half of 2018. As a regulation it will be implemented directly, replacing the current divergent national laws based on the EU Data Protection Directive of 1995 and in so doing creating a more harmonized data protection landscape. There are a number of key areas within the landscape which we should consider.

Informed consent remains the foundation for data processing

The essence of data protection legislation is to ensure that personal data is only to be gathered and used by businesses (as data controllers or data processors in data protection terms) on specified lawful grounds. The GDPR extends the understanding of personal data, which is any information 'relating to' an individual, to specifically include online identifiers such as cookies and advertising IDs used extensively in the online and mobile world. These will now be considered to be personal data, along with anything that contributes to identifying an individual, or links to such identifying information. Additionally special categories of personal data which require explicit consent have been expanded to include biometric and genetic data along with data such as race, health, sexual life, criminal offences, religious beliefs and political opinion and trade union membership.

From a research perspective, the most important of the lawful grounds for processing data will continue to be informed consent. By gaining clear consent from individuals to process their data, researchers can develop and build trust. The social contract between research practitioners and research participants relies on informed consent and respect for the rights and well-being of individuals. The importance of recognizing and reiterating this in robust data practices is reflected in the new legal framework. The GDPR introduces a higher consent bar, requiring freely given, specific and informed consent demonstrated through clear affirmative action. A key part of the test of valid consent is whether individuals actually understand what they are agreeing to, and are given a meaningful choice. This focus on securing informed and transparent consent is reflected in the sector's various codes of practice/conduct for research, such as the MRS *Code of Conduct*.

There are other grounds for businesses to process the data of individuals, such as on the basis of their legitimate interests. Using this ground is a balancing act which must take into account the reasonable expectations of data subjects and should be conducted in line with compatible purposes. As research is expressly considered to be a compatible purpose for data use, research can legally be carried out on customer databases on this ground. The GDPR also continues a research exemption (if allowed by national law) which will allow data to be processed, where no other ground is feasible, and technical and security safeguards such as encryption or 'pseudonymization', ie de-identification of the data, have been put in place.

Giving control to people by focusing on the data subject

Facilitating the control by individuals over their personal data is a pivotal part of the comprehensive overhaul of the law. The new and enhanced individual rights, over this wider notion of personal data, are the foundation of the new regime.

These include:

- New right to be forgotten or 'right of erasure' which codifies recent European case law and allows individuals to request that personal data, made public especially in online environments, be erased. Businesses will still be able to process the data if there are compelling legitimate grounds for processing to continue, but are obliged to inform other businesses who may be processing the data to delete it if this request is received.

- New right of data portability will allow individuals to request that their data be provided in a usable, transferable format, allowing them to move data between platforms or suppliers. This right will apply where the personal data details have been collected by automated means on the basis of an individual's consent or contract.

- New right, albeit of a more limited impact, to request that data processing is restricted, especially where the data cannot be deleted, such as where it is required for legal reasons.

- New general right to be informed about significant data breaches. Serious data breaches must be notified to the data protection authority and if the breach presents a risk to individuals (such as identity fraud) they must also be directly told about the breach.

CASE STUDY 1   Mydex

Businesses that enable individuals to take control of their data, empowering individuals to be more confident participants of the 21st-century digital data economy, are essential for a balanced social contract between business and individuals; and will be crucial for the forthcoming legislative changes to have the desired outcome.

In this case study, Mydex, a Fair Data enabler, sets out its role in enabling individuals to take control.

Mydex is a Community Interest Company. It is asset locked. It serves individuals by helping them manage their lives more effectively through provision of tools and services that let them collect, accumulate, organize, analyse and share the data about their lives — whether this is data that organizations hold about them, that they generate themselves, or is generated around them through daily living. Fair Data certification is an important external indicator of our commitment.

Personal data is valuable, and personal control over personal data requires both transparency and trust. Mydex's mission as a Community Interest Company and operator of a Trust Framework and secure platform is to demonstrate this internally and externally. Certification as a Fair Data Company and the first certified Fair Data Enabler is an important external measure of trust, as is our ISO 27001 certification for information security management.

Connecting to the Mydex Platform also delivers benefits to businesses, their customers and the long term relationship they have with each other. It reduces friction in customer journeys, effort for the customer and the organization, and back-office costs in terms of verification, data logistics and achieving compliance.

Mydex acts as a neutral, non-competing, public service platform, and is designed to embed trust in all transactions and interactions between organizations and those they service and support.

Connecting Mydex to existing systems and services is easy and the entire customer journey and brand experience remains with connecting organizations.

Mydex enables organizations to open up new channels of engagement, support omni-channels more easily and access a broader, richer set of timely and accurate information about customers, secure better insights and achieve easier personal-ization of services at the same time as assisting in achieving Fair Data certification.

Strengthened right to object to direct marketing

Individuals have a right to object to profiling and not to be subject to decisions based on automated processing. The profiling activities that are relevant here are those done through automated processing where a decision is made that has legal or significant effects on individuals. Importantly, this will not cover research activities such as segmentation, as these are not designed to have legal impact directly on individuals. There is also an absolute right to object to processing for direct marketing and profiling for direct marketing without being required to provide specific reasons.

Enhanced information rights

Information rights have been significantly enhanced. Individuals must be given a far greater amount of processing information, such as the source of the data and the period for which the data will be held. The information also has to be provided in an intelligible form and using clear accessible language. Interestingly. there is now a duty on businesses to promote all of these rights to individuals.

Alongside these new substantive rights are procedural rights which mean that if authorities do not act then individuals can (on their own or with representation) as can consumer protection groups (if allowed by national law).

Underpinning the strengthened individual rights is one of the key features of the GDPR, namely that it will have extraterritorial application. All organizations processing the personal data of EU residents will be required to comply with the provisions of the regulation, regardless as to where the business is located. Businesses which offer goods or services across borders, or monitor activities of EU subjects, will now be covered by EU data protection laws.

Accountability obligations

Businesses will no longer be required to notify or register with their national data protection authority. However, this bureaucratic requirement will be replaced with more detailed requirements on businesses, such as ensuring full record keeping of processing activities, conducting privacy impact assessments and embedding privacy by design and default throughout the business. For research practitioners it will be pivotal to use organizational technical and security safeguards, such as de-identified or 'pseudonymized' data. This is still personal data, but it is a mechanism for minimizing risk.

Increased obligations on data processors, which previously had fewer statutory obligations, mean that the risk profile of data processors such as transcribers, storage providers and recruiters has been raised considerably. This is in part because their role meant that they did not determine the purposes for which the data will be used. Researchers of all sizes and involved in all types of activities, from panel research to qualitative focus groups and quantitative surveys to data analytics, will need to take steps to become fully data protection compliant. Guidance from national and European data protection authorities, as well as the European Commission, will shape the precise manner in which the technical rules in the finalized framework are enforced. MRS will interpret these, looking specifically how they apply in the research context, to assist researchers across all areas of research in understanding their obligations.

CASE STUDY 2   Ark Data

The strengthening of regulators' powers, the huge increase in sanctions, and the increased obligations being placed on businesses across all touch points in the data journey, will mean that those businesses and organizations that invest in robust, well-managed processes, with partners they can trust to deliver, will be crucial for staying on the right side of the new legislation.

Here Ark Data, a Fair Data accredited company, sets out how they help businesses keep their data up-to-date.

Your data might be secure but is it up to date?

Many businesses spend vast amounts of time and money ensuring their data is secure. But what about the quality and accuracy of that customer data?

In the UK over 500,000 people die and more than 6 million people move home every year. Customer data decays rapidly and not doing anything about it can be risky:

- Assuming the identity of the deceased is the easiest way to commit fraud (currently estimated at over £52 billion per annum).

- Mailing the deceased causes upset to the bereaved, leaves brands open to criticism by the media (think of what happened to the charity sector last year) and is expensive and wasteful.

- Internal analysis and reporting using out-of-date and inaccurate customer data means businesses are working on potentially dangerous information.

The Ark is a data quality business that owns and publishes two data products: the **National Deceased Register (NDR)** and a 'gone away' suppression file called **Re-mover**. NDR is a database used by our licensees to identify and remove customers and prospects who have died from their own databases and lists. Re-mover does exactly the same but for customers and prospects who have moved home.

The Ark's clients span many sectors including financial services (banking and insurance), retail, charity, utilities and mail order. The Ark is a **Fair Data**™-accredited organization and its people are passionate about raising the profile of data quality, working hard to encourage compliance with best practice in data suppression and adherence to the Fair Data principles.

The Ark offers a **free data audit service** to help businesses understand the weaknesses in their data and show how we can help businesses avoid unnecessary risks involved with relying on inaccurate data that could lead to potentially expensive outcomes.

High sanctions are part of the enforcement toolkit

Data protection authorities have been given a much wider range of powers for enforcement of the data protection rules. The new level of administrative fines have grabbed the headlines and are significant. Penalties currently imposed in different jurisdictions of the EU pale in comparison to the new approach. For example, the highest penalty previously imposed in the UK is £350,000; in Germany it is €1.1 million and in France €150,000. All of these fines are much lower than the maximum allowed penalties under the new law of up to 4 per cent of worldwide turnover or €20 million. In addition to fines, the authorities also have greater investigative powers to compel information from businesses and gain access to premises.

Shaping the new social contract

Compliance needs to be placed at the core of operations by enshrining privacy by design as a default. This goes hand in hand with the recognition of the social contract and the value exchange for data that powers the digital economy.

In this new environment it is critical that data-intensive business, such as research, continues to demonstrate respect for individual rights and enshrine this within their business operation. Adopting an approach that embeds privacy at all stages and all touch points in the data journey – from collection through to analysis and reporting – should be the overriding and primary consideration for businesses. As awareness of data protections and rights increases, the commercial implications and reputational impact means that focus across all industries on securing consumer and customer trust will accelerate.

So where do we go from here?

The growing sense of imbalance in the data-sharing relationship between individuals and business, the deterioration in trust, the commoditization of personal data and the increasing legislative environment all point to a more complex data environment – so what can we do?

Fair Data

In January 2013, MRS launched a new ethical consumer mark for personal data, called Fair Data. The trust mark means that members of the public are able to easily identify between those organizations that collect, use and retain personal data properly and ethically, and those that do not (and is more of a 'carrot' approach to data compliance).

As can be seen from the research, consumers gravitate towards companies they trust. Recognized ethical marks help consumers make choices, separating trustworthy brands with those which share their values. This has been learned from other industries such as Fairtrade, Investors in People (IIP), recycling symbols and so on. Launched for all those organizations – public and private sector – that collect and use personal data, Fair Data is becoming a recognizable standard for organizations that can be trusted to do the right thing with individuals' data. It has been designed to be used internationally, integrating and complementing business-to-business initiatives like the data transfer arrangements such as binding contracts, the US/EU Privacy Shield and the Data Seal of Approval initiative in Europe. Fair Data has also been exported to other markets, such as Singapore.

FIGURE 10.1   The role of fair data in corporate responsibility

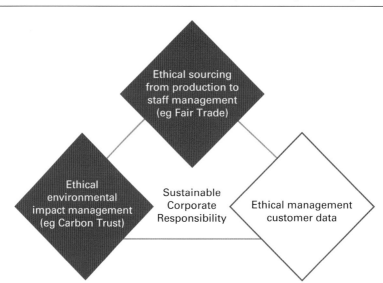

Fair Data uses ten principles based on rules from the MRS *Code of Conduct*, and data protection legislation, which have been re-positioned to aid consumers' understanding of their rights and organizations' obligations in terms of protecting their personal data.

By signing up to be a Fair Data organization, organizations agree to: adhere to the Fair Data principles and to use the Fair Data mark in all relevant dealings with customers and participants.

By creating a seemingly simple approach of ten principles, the scheme can be easily understood by a wide range of organizations. To highlight this, two different organizations – personal data store Community Interest Company Mydex, and data quality specialists Ark Data – explained in the case studies why they become Fair Data accredited.

However, for all its perceived simplicity, the accreditation is a robust all-encompassing approach. Through the ten principles all minimum legislative requirements have been covered, and in addition broader ethical requirements including the ethical treatment of vulnerable citizens, and ethical supply chain management and procurement are incorporated. Table 10.1 summarizes the ten principles demonstrating the higher standards that are being met by those organizations that have achieved Fair Data accreditation.

Fair Data is a unique innovation, which addresses an issue that is impacting business, society and citizens. Fair Data is the only data trust mark scheme

TABLE 10.1　Fair Data Principles

Data Topic	Fair Data Principles
Consent	1　We will ensure that all personal data is collected with customers' consent.
Data use, retention and quality	2　We will not use personal data for any purpose other than that for which consent was given, respecting customers' wishes about the use of their data.
Data access	3　We will make sure that customers have access to their personal data that we hold, and that we tell them how we use it
Data security and transfer	4　We will protect personal data and keep it secure and confidential.
Protection/avoidance of harm	5　We will ensure staff understand that personal data is just that – personal – and ensure that it is treated with respect.
Vulnerable adults and children	6　We will ensure that the vulnerable and under-age are properly protected by the processes we use for data collection.
Clients, suppliers and the supply-chain	7　We will manage our data supply chain to the same ethical standards we expect from other suppliers. 8　We will ensure that ethical best practice in personal data is integral to our procurement process.
Staff training	9　We will ensure that all staff who have access to personal data are properly trained in its use.
Professional reputation	10　We will not use personal data if there is uncertainty as to whether the Fair Data Principles have been applied.

to receive support from the UK's data protection regulator, the Information Commissioner. It is a scheme that brings all constituencies together, and embeds trust, in a world where the digital data economy is the driving force for businesses, society and citizens. Fair Data has also been recognized more widely, including winning Best Innovation at the Association Excellence awards 2015.

Conclusion

For business, the Corporate Social Responsibility agenda is becoming increasingly important as brands strive to differentiate themselves.

This is not about businesses being legal: for any brand or business to survive it needs, as an absolute minimum, to meet its legal obligations. But as the public becomes more wary of data issues, the brands that thrive will be those that put ethical, customer-centric business practices at their core. With Fair Data, MRS is providing a framework to help businesses to do this.

Research studies such as Orange's *Future of Digital Trust* report highlight that opportunities exist for those organizations and businesses that are intelligent, consensual and responsible in their use of consumer data, with trustworthy data use becoming increasingly a fundamental requirement, which will have a significant impact on companies' overall reputations. Equally, as the public become more mindful of sharing their personal data, the effect could have long-term implications for businesses and society.

There is clear value for business in not only *saying* the right things, but *doing* the right things. But to be responsible – to be trusted and meaningful – requires not only investment in processes and procedures, but a fundamental re-think about data. Technology enables businesses to do amazing things; what is often forgotten, however, is the question of whether they should be doing these 'amazing things'! What looks like a transformative data technology approach to a business can look scary and intrusive to a customer.

In the words of Andreas Koller, 'Data is people in disguise.'[10] Businesses need to re-orient their thinking about data; yes it it is Big Data, Smart Data, Actionable Data, Insightful Data, or however else you wish to describe it, but data *is* people. Treat the data as you would the human. Think of data in the same way as if the human behind the data were standing in front of you. The businesses and organizations that are able to put this 'human' data mindset at the heart of what they do, will be the ones that gain the trust of people, and will be the ones that flourish. Researchers, with their exceptional skills understanding people, are uniquely placed to serve as the bridge between organizations and their data, giving people a voice for the benefit of all.

References

1 IBM www-01.ibm.com/software/data/bigdata/what-is-big-data.html

2 IBM www.ibmbigdatahub.com/infographic/four-vs-big-data

3 *Social Media Today* www.socialmediatoday.com/social-networks/kadie-regan/2015-08-10/10-amazing-social-media-growth-stats-2015

4 Facebook http://newsroom.fb.com/company-info/

5 Office for National Statistics: http://www.ons.gov.uk/ons/rel/crime-stats/crime-statistics/year-ending-june-2015/index.html

6 KPMG https://assets.kpmg.com/content/dam/kpmg/pdf/2016/02/small-business-reputation-new.pdf

7 Europa http://ec.europa.eu/public_opinion/archives/eb_special_439_420_en.htm#431

8 GRBN http://grbn.org/trust/

9 Orange http://www.orange.com/en/content/download/25973/581975/version/2/file/Report+-+My+Data+Value+-+Orange+Future+of+Digital+Trust+-+FINAL.pdf

10 Andreas Koller: http://blog.andreaskoller.com/2014/02/data-is-people-in-disguise/ [7 February 2014]